Mirth of a Nation

15 years of humour in the **Mail & Guardian**

This selection © **Mail & Guardian**

ISBN 0 620 26033 5

First published in 2000
by **M&G Books**
a division of
M&G Media
Media Mill
7 Quince Road
Milpark 2092
Website: www.mg.co.za

Cover and layout design by
Disturbance
15 Hammersmith Avenue
Berea
Durban 4001
e-mail : disturb@mweb.co.za

Printed by
Formset Printers
22/23 Kinghall Avenue
Eppindust
Cape Town 7640

Contents

Part Three: The Body Electric

Part Four: The Body Politic

Part Five: Cultural Weapons

Part Six: Change Is Pain

Foreword

The Mail & Guardian: An Appreciation
Irwin Manoim
Joint Founder and Editor, 1985-94

Every Friday morning for the past 15 years, discerning South African newspaper readers have looked forward to the nuanced pleasures of balanced journalism, meticulous reporting, erudite analysis, the opinions of some of our leading citizens and the polished wit of sophisticated columnists. On the other hand, these same discerning *Business Day* readers could, for just a few bucks more, have purchased the *Mail & Guardian*, a scurrilous runt of a rag with a knack for pissing off every last decent, upstanding South African.

Business Day, like any nourishing cereal, is read over breakfast to calm the nerves, stimulate the synapses and relax the bowels in preparation for the day ahead. *The Mail & Guardian* is read over breakfast to palpitate the ventricles, to encourage disgorgement, sweaty palms, tics to the eye and exaggerated vocal activity, in preparation for the task ahead, namely the composition of a letter on the lines of "Dear Sir or Madam or Whatever you call yourself, I have just flung today's edition of your once-enlightened newspaper into the bin, because I can no longer bear to be confronted each Friday morning by the puerile and illiterate scribblings of that so-called, sexist, crypto-intellectual ..."

Which raises a philosophical question. What is the best way to avoid reading the *Mail & Guardian*? Many people try the camouflage trick, which is to buy another newspaper and look innocent, but that's not nearly as effective as buying a subscription to the *Mail & Guardian*, which will then, for the next two years, be unfailingly delivered to a wide selection of your neighbours, but rarely to you.

What kind of people would even consider exposing themselves to the torrents of bile spewed weekly by the *Mail & Guardian*? Distinguished people, as it happens, people like Thabo Mbeki, or Barney Pityana, or John Berks. Here's what our president himself has to say: "Each Friday morning I wait eagerly at the front door to watch my rolled-up *Mail & Guardian* waft over the security fence and land on the boerbul. The nuanced pleasures of your balanced journalism, meticulous reporting and erudite analysis provide a sensuous frisson that has at times driven me to raptures. The opinions expressed in your delightful journal play a central role in influencing the policies of this government, and I have taken the liberty of ordering a special gift subscription for Robert Mugabe."*

The editors of this inexpensive volume have requested an abbreviated history of the newspaper, touching on a few of the highlights, such as they are. The newspaper, first called *The Weekly Mail*, was begun in 1985 by human flotsam from the recently expired *Rand Daily Mail* and *Sunday Express*. The *Weekly Mail* was intended to fill a gap in the market, as the newspaper for people who worry a lot, providing them each week with hitherto unexplored terrain for anxiety. *Weekly Mail* readers were the first in South Africa to learn that their underarm sprays had caused the hole in the ozone layer, their tuna salads the death of the oceans, and their BMWs Third World debt. There were also rich pickings in the rape of Papua New Guinea, Eritrea and East Timor, global capitalism (greed of), female orgasms (infrequency of), Afghan women (shopping, dearth of), white men (rhythm, not much), genetically modified foods, elephants and whales, rain forests, and of course, PW Botha.

*In keeping with Mail & Guardian policy, a middle-aged white editor has made certain enhancements to the original quote.

The paper also provided an outlet for oft-neglected words like deconstructivism or post-colonial or archetypal or disjuncture. The upside for the *Weekly Mail* reader was the paper's guidance in situations where worrying was inappropriate, for example when the eldest daughter shacked up with a Rasta, grandad ran off with another man and the maid joined the Socialist Workers Party.

After the first issue was published in June 1985, the few pundits to notice predicted that *The Weekly Mail* would be bankrupt in a month, which it was. Why it is still with us 15 years later is a mystery, particularly to the staff of Nedbank, Braamfontein, whose role in the unexpected survival of this important cultural product has been little acknowledged.

Early on the paper developed a knack for annoying persons of substance, who expressed their displeasure in diverse ways. The less imaginative merely issued writs; the more inventive experimented with Molotov cocktails, rocks through windows, police batons and speeches on prime-time TV. The current editor still has bullet shards rattling around inside his skull, which are said to explain his erratic behaviour, although only by those who didn't know him before he got shot. The paper was banned at various times, but long-suffering readers rarely noticed, taking it for granted that once again it had just not been delivered.

Lightness of touch was not one of the hallmarks of the old *Weekly Mail*. Asked to summarise its most significant traits, an unbiased observer might have remarked perhaps on its greyness, longwindedness, exhausting depressingness, and its ability, even in the face of overwhelming reasons for optimism, to always find something to niggle about. One prominent TV critic was quietly axed when his reviews betrayed faint hints of enjoyment. The movie critics were allowed greater flexibility, and could admire directors whose names were polysyllabic and contained no vowels. The literary critics practised such advanced forms of erudition that it was less trouble to read an entire 400-page book than figure out the 400-word review.

Despite the aforementioned, the editors of this inexpensive volume, Barbara Ludman and Shaun de Waal, have devoted months to archival research in the coffee shops of Johannesburg's northern suburbs, uncovering a trove of unexpected gems. There's the wayward priest Thomas Equinus, steeped in Marxist and horseracing lore; know-all Krisjan Lemmer, liar of the Marico; the *Dear Walter* letters, suspected by some to be faked; the first *Madam and Eve* cartoons, and much more. The usual South African criteria have been applied to the final published selection: nepotism, prejudice, personal enmity, cronyism and backhanders. It is not for me to point fingers, but none of the three distinguished editors of this newspaper has been represented in keeping with his station.

With the death of apartheid in 1994, many observers believed that the querulous and carping *Mail & Guardian* would cease to have a role. It is therefore a tribute to the efforts of the current staff that the *Mail & Guardian* becomes more offensive with each passing week, encouraged no doubt by the close correlation between the number of people who phone to cancel their subscriptions each Friday morning and the number of extra newspapers sold.

Finally, a word of appreciation to those people whose untiring contributions behind the scenes made this slim volume possible: Adriaan Vlok, Stoffel Botha, Louis Luyt, Winnie Mandela, Magnus Malan, Magnus Heystek, Marthinus van Schalkwyk, Emanuel Shaw II, Craig Williamson, Mangosuthu Buthelezi, and many more: our thanks to each and every one of you.

Introduction

Smile out loud
Shaun de Waal and Barbara Ludman

"We're putting together a volume of humorous writing from the *Mail* to celebrate our 15th anniversary."

"A very slim volume, then?"

The reader will note that *Mirth of a Nation* is not particularly slim. This is because we've expanded the ordinary definition of what is humorous: not just the laugh-out-loud, slipping-on-banana-peels, guffawing-till-you-weep sort of pieces, but writing with wit, writing with a sly undercurrent of irony. And there has been plenty of that in *The Weekly Mail* and the *Mail & Guardian* over the past decade and a half.

In the early years, many readers loved (and some hated) *Letters from a Linksfield Liberal*, which ran for 18 months (we include the very first of them), until one of the writers left the country – as did the Linksfield Liberal himself. The Liberal emigrated to Britain (or was it Bulgaria?) because co-author Debra Aarons got a Fulbright scholarship and went off to Boston to do her PhD. By the time she came back, seven years later, there was a new government.

Worm's Eye View, by Steven Friedman, began its life in the *Rand Daily Mail* and carried over to its bastard child, *The Weekly Mail*. A column of satirical political commentary, it developed even more bizarre tendencies in the mid-Eighties, no doubt as a result of the pressures of the surreal South African political situation. The Republic of ParaNoya, indeed.

The horseracing column, written by a divinity student at the University of the Witwatersrand, could have no byline but Thomas Equinus. It was one of the most popular columns the paper ever published, read by people with no interest whatsoever in horseracing – although the betting tips were pretty good, too. In this collection, we have removed the tips from the tail-end of the column; now they are entirely irrelevant, rather than just largely irrelevant. The column was so popular that Equinus (in reality Jeff Zerbst) parlayed some of his regular themes into a successful live cabaret at the hip Black Sun nightspot. Zerbst got his theology doctorate eventually, and went on to edit pornographic magazines in South Africa and Australia.

In his television columns, Gus Silber applied his unflagging and apparently effortless sense of humour to a wide variety of morbid symptoms of the interregnum as they appeared on the box. He was followed as television columnist by Charlotte Bauer, whose finely tuned sense of irony picked out the most absurd elements of life on the small screen. She also wrote general arts features and interviews, many of which were as entertaining as her television column.

Man-about-town Thami Mkhwanazi came to *The Weekly Mail* straight from a Robben Island cell, and paused only briefly before launching a tour of some of the country's better shebeens and nightspots; his witty and sophisticated columns made many watering holes famous.

In later years, as *The Weekly Mail* evolved into *The Weekly Mail & Guardian* and then, finally, lost the "weekly" altogether, readers were entertained by columnists such as Robert Kirby (who became the paper's television columnist in 1999) and David Beresford. The latter was the uncredited author of what purported to be letters to Walter Sisulu from Nelson Mandela himself – a secret revealed with the publication of a successful collection of *Dear Walter* columns.

The secret of who writes the column under the *nom de plume* of Krisjan Lemmer – "the biggest liar in the bosveld" – has, however, never been revealed, and for good reason: there have been at least five different journalists posing as Krisjan since the column began in the late 1980s. It continues to be one of the most popular features of the newspaper; we have scattered some Lemmers throughout the book.

Angella Johnson arrived at the *Mail & Guardian* from London. Born in Jamaica, grown to feisty adulthood in Britain, she'd come to South Africa briefly in 1994 to cover the elections and then – intrigued at the possibility of finding her African roots – returned. She stayed for a couple of years, delighted *M&G* readers, then went back to London.

Film-maker and playwright John Matshikiza came home, after most of a lifetime abroad, and stayed long enough to share with *M&G* readers the discoveries he was making about living in Johannesburg's northern suburbs and, later, in the less salubrious but no less fascinating corners of the country.

Fine reporters discovered a talent for mockery – and self-mockery – in the *M&G*. Mercedes Sayagues, the *M&G*'s Zimbabwe correspondent, has been dashing off tales of her unsuccessful romantic encounters between examples of standard *M&G* fare: politics, poverty and war.

In the early days, arts writer Ivor Powell brought a razor wit and a certain delight to bear on subjects ranging from commune living to censorship, before he moved on to the weightier and less obviously humorous area of politics. His interest in corruption, however, has continued through the years, and has lately been shared by several colleagues, including Jubie Matlou and, especially, Evidence wa ka Ngobeni.

Early *Weekly Mail* readers also had the chance to contribute some humour to the paper in a forum other than the letters page when, in 1985, the *Mail* ran a competition soliciting captions for odd pictures. The photo to be seen in this book, one of Pik Botha cooking something mysterious in a large pot, drew the most hilarious entries.

The *Mail* has had superb cartoonists. The wild arabesques of Derek Bauer's savage political cartoons, which perfectly captured the spirit of the era, were first published in *The Weekly Mail*. So was *Madam and Eve*, the first domestic cartoon strip to compare with international strips in quality of wit and sheer professionalism of graphics.

In this volume, we reproduce the very first *Madam and Eve* cartoon, which appeared in mid-1992, as well as one from the following year. The same team is responsible for *Chalkdust*, which enlivens the pages of the *M&G's* sister publication *The Teacher*. Back in the late Eighties and early Nineties, Stacey Stent's series *Who's Left* gently and wryly mocked the left-leaning lifestyle – social commentary that was perfect for the pages of *The Weekly Mail*. At present, Zapiro (Jonathan Shapiro) is the paper's chief cartoonist; his unfailingly accurate political instinct and grip of post-apartheid politics make his weekly cartoon, which sits opposite the leaders, worth well over a thousand words of analysis. Dr Jack (Jack Swanepoel) is the *M&G's* signature. His graphics are found throughout the newspaper, on all subjects, from technology to education – and politics.

Apart from its writers and cartoonists, the *Mail* has upheld a proud tradition of wit in its headlines and front pages (the latter, until 1994, the work of Irwin Manoim). In the early days, the paper displayed a flamboyant chutzpah that reflected the need to defy authority, and we have included a set of front pages that embody that aim. Now the *Mail & Guardian* is older, though not perhaps any wiser, and embroiled in new political controversies – ones without the clarity provided by apartheid. Still, we make an effort to laugh, to make the reader laugh, as often as we can; failing that, the least we can do is attempt to make you smile out loud.

THE WEEKLY MAIL

PRICES: JOHANNESBURG, PRETORIA & REEF R1,00 (plus 12c GST) — ELSEWHERE IN SA R1,12 (excl.) GST)

Volume 2, Number 24. FRIDAY JUNE 20 to THURSDAY JUNE 26, 1986

THE PAPER FOR A CHANGING SOUTH AFRICA

WE'RE BACK ON THE STREETS!
The paper that was seized last week will be on sale as usual from today

The EPG report: An extraordinary document made ordinary by our extraordinary times **8**

A leaf-munching plan to beat malnutrition **7**

FRONT PAGE COMMENT

Our lawyers tell us we can say almost nothing critical about the Emergency

But we'll try:

Pɪᴋ BOTHA, the Minister of Foreign Affairs, told US television audiences this week that the South African press remained free.

We hope that ▮▮▮▮▮▮▮▮▮▮▮▮▮▮▮▮▮▮ ▮▮▮▮▮▮▮▮▮▮▮▮▮▮▮▮▮▮▮▮▮▮▮▮, was listening.

They considered our publication subversive.
● If it is subversive to speak out against ▮▮▮▮▮, we plead guilty.
● If it is subversive to express concern about ▮▮▮▮▮, we plead guilty.
● If it is subversive to believe that there are better routes to peace than the ▮▮▮▮▮▮, we plead guilty.

● To PAGE 2

RESTRICTED Reports on these pages have been censored to comply with Emergency regulations

THE WEEKLY MAIL

PRICES:
WITWATERSRAND & PRETORIA R1.00 (incl. GST) | ELSEWHERE IN SA R1.12 (incl. GST)

VOLUME 3, NUMBER 33, FRIDAY AUGUST 21 to THURSDAY AUGUST 27, 1987

THE PAPER FOR A CHANGING SOUTH AFRICA

MY YEARS ON THE ISLAND
Thami Mkhwanazi continues his remarkable series about life on Robben Island
PAGE 16

EXCLUSIVE:

The State President's master plan

to combat the revolutionary onslaught

THE State President has called upon the press to help combat the revolutionary onslaught which threatens the country.

We are happy to oblige:

⦿ By continuing to expose the injustices of apartheid.

⦿ By continuing to report points of view which his government chooses to ignore.

⦿ By continuing to push for democracy instead of minority rule

The State President has accused the press of negative reporting. We assure him we are happy to report on his positive actions.

Lately, we haven't seen any.

---

7 000 miners face sacking

Thousands queue for last pay at marginal mine that's been shut

By JO-ANN BEKKER

MORE than 7 000 black miners are facing dismissal rather than break South Africa's largest strike ever, which ends its second week today.

About 3 000 gold miners from Anglo's Vaal Reef's No 6 shaft, who defied management's warnings to return to work or face closure of the marginal mine, queued all yesterday to receive their final payments.

And according to the National Union of Mineworkers, about 4 000 workers from Anglo's Western Holdings No 1 shaft were preparing to follow suit. They were expected to prepare to go home, notwithstanding Anglo's threat to close the marginal shaft if they did not return to work by this morning.

In a related development, the NUM claimed about 24 000 workers at four Gencor mines in Evander had been ordered to return to work by last night or lose their jobs. This was denied by Gencor.

Earlier this week the NUM tried to persuade striking miners to return to work in marginal shafts — as these unproductive or low-grade mines would naturally be the first to be closed during a strike.

PUTTING A PRICE ON THE STRIKE
PAGE 6

About 700 workers on Amcoal's Landau colliery — scheduled to be closed in March — chose to resume work on Tuesday to avert the mine's immediate closure. Cyril Ramaphosa, NUM general secretary, said he respected the decision as it had been taken democratically by workers.

Nevertheless, a NUM representative said the decision by the 7 000 workers at the Vaal Reef and Western Holdings shafts to lose their jobs rather than break the strike signalled worker determination and support for the wage strike.

A Gencor representative — responding to the NUM's claims that Evander workers had been given an ultimatum to return to work or be fired — denied the union's claims. He said that, as was the "accepted practice", workers had been informed they were "absent from work without permission" and failure to return to work by yesterday would result in disciplinary hearings.

NUM queried the basis for Gencor's threat and reiterated that the strike was legal.

This week began with signs of a thaw in the cold war between strikers and mine owners which has characterised the strike since it began on Sunday night, August 9. On Monday, the NUM accepted Anglo's offer to discuss mine violence, which has claimed one life and injured about 300 workers in the first 11 days of the strike.

But the following day NUM walked out of the talks in protest before they had reached any resolution, after hearing 15 strikers at the entrance to the President Steyn Gold Mine had been injured by police firing rubber bullets and wielding sjamboks.

⦿ To PAGE 2

THE
WEEKLY MAIL

The paper for a changing South Africa

R2,20 (R1,95 + 25c GST) ★Southern Africa: R2,20 excl. tax

Vol. 7, No. 29. July 26 to August 1 1991

The search for the sex-starved, radioactive goats
Our special section on science and technology uncovers some curious quirks   PAGE 19

The artists in the flying taxis
A taxi-driver argues eloquently that he and his wild colleagues are sorely misunderstood   PAGE 7

A chemical war on the factory floor
Our monthly focus on green issues looks at chemical hazards in the work place   PAGE 7

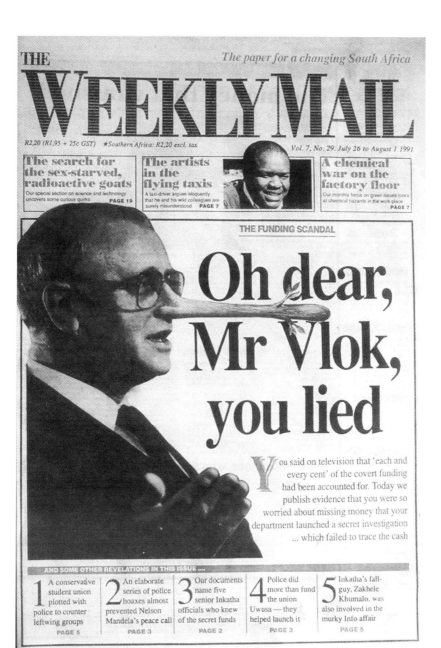

THE FUNDING SCANDAL

Oh dear, Mr Vlok, you lied

You said on television that 'each and every cent' of the covert funding had been accounted for. Today we publish evidence that you were so worried about missing money that your department launched a secret investigation ... which failed to trace the cash

AND SOME OTHER REVELATIONS IN THIS ISSUE ...

1 A conservative student union plotted with police to counter leftwing groups   PAGE 5

2 An elaborate series of police hoaxes almost prevented Nelson Mandela's peace call   PAGE 3

3 Our documents name five senior Inkatha officials who knew of the secret funds   PAGE 2

4 Police did more than fund the union Uwusa — they helped launch it   PAGE 3

5 Inkatha's fall-guy, Zakhele Khumalo, was also involved in the murky Info affair   PAGE 5

THE WEEKLY MAIL

PRICES: WITWATERSRAND & PRETORIA R1,00 (incl. GST) | ELSEWHERE IN SA R1,12 (incl. GST)

Final instalment in our popular series...
MY LIFE AS A MINER
This week: STRIKE!
PAGE 12

VOLUME 4, NUMBER 31. FRIDAY AUGUST 19 to THURSDAY AUGUST 25, 1988

THE PAPER FOR A CHANGING SOUTH AFRICA

The lonely prisoner of Nelson Mandela

He loses if he frees the ANC leader. He loses if he doesn't

FREE PW!

Swapo's Nujoma speaks: No ANC bases in Namibia

As Namibia moves to independence, an interview with Swapo president SAM NUJOMA

DAVID NIDDRIE
reports from Lusaka

SWAPO will not provide military bases in Namibia from which the African National Congress can strike into South Africa.

Neither does it intend substantial nationalisation of Namibian industry, much of it South African-owned, nor to appropriate white farmland, a move it believes could stampede the 75 000 whites into exile.

Instead the South West African People's Organisation will seek as cordial a relationship as possible with its former colonial rulers as it attempts to establish the basis of an independent national economy.

This is the message from Swapo's president, Sam Nujoma. Nujoma is in Kabwe, Zambia, this week to attend the 23rd congress of Zambia's United National Independence Party (UNIP) — where several thousand delegates and observers are reviewing the consequences of their own governments' post-independence attempt to nationalise South African-owned mines.

He and senior members of Swapo have outlined the policies Swapo will adopt when it becomes the first government of an independent Namibia — as Nujoma is supremely confident it will and even his enemies accept is likely.

● To PAGE 2

Swapo's Sam Nujoma ... in search of cordial relations with South Africa
Picture: PAUL WEINBERG, Afrapix

PW BOTHA can't bring himself to free Nelson Mandela; but he also can't hold him forever.

That the State President is a prisoner of the situation, unable to move in either direction, was made clear yesterday in Botha's speech to the Natal Congress of the National Party in Durban.

He can't keep the African National Congress leader in prison indefinitely because it is increasingly apparent that international pressure will continue and there will be little prospect for progress in his government's "reform" policies. Black leaders, including most of the moderates, have made Mandela's release a precondition for participating in the "reform" process.

On the other hand, Botha fears the unpredictable result of releasing Mandela, particularly when the crucial October municipal elections are only two months away.

Mandela's illness this week brought home the danger of the 70-year-old resistance leader dying in prison. That prospect — and the likelihood of severe repercussions — must be why Botha broke from his prepared speech yesterday to address the issue for the second day in a row.

It may also account for the noticeably softer tone adopted by Botha.

Earlier this week, in an extraordinary reply to a letter from Frank Chikane, South African Council of Churches general-secretary, Botha said Mandela was a "special" prisoner and that he was "even more concerned" with Mandela's health than was the SACC.

And yesterday, Botha told the Natal Congress: "Personally I don't think that at his age and condition it would be wise for him to choose to go back to prison and I hope he will make it possible for me to act in a humane way so that we can have peace in South Africa."

This attitude was taken even further by Information Minister Dr Stoffel van der Merwe at a Pretoria press function.

The government would like to see Mandela released from prison, Van Der Merwe said. There was no reason why the South African government should keep him in jail.

The level of government concern was shown by the fact that Minister of Justice Kobie Coetsee personally visited Mandela in hospital on Wednesday.

Botha may have softened his tone, but he reiterated his condition for Mandela's release: that he renounce violence as a political weapon and undertake not to campaign for the process of violence in South Africa.

Mandela has repeatedly made it clear he won't play along with this. He won't renounce

● To PAGE 2

> **World pressure to free Mandela. But the Right could score in October**
> By ANTON HARBER, CARMEL RICKARD and GAYE DAVIS

The contents of this newspaper have been restricted in terms of the Emergency regulations

Part One
States of Emergency

Letters from a Linksfield Liberal
Debra Aarons, Anton Harber, Barbara Ludman

"Mon-Imali"
Linksfield
Johannesburg

My Son,

It's time you came home. I can't face this crazy country alone any longer.

Take last Friday night. We sit down to watch the television news – myself, your mother, your grandmother, your uncle Harry, your sister Gloria, and a seven-foot-tall Rastafarian your sister Gloria found in the Wits canteen during her Soc Anthro II (repeat) lecture. Just an ordinary happy family (one breadwinner, 17 dependants, 42 cars, a Kreepy Krauly and a compact disc player) trying to get on with life behind an eight-foot wall in the northern suburbs.

An ordinary family – but this was no ordinary Friday night.

First, they come on television to tell us that PW has ticked off Pik because Pik promised us a black state president by the end of next week.

Your grandmother has chosen not to notice your sister Gloria's boyfriend. She backs PW all the way: "Quite right. You know how they pinch the sugar."

The Rasta, pouring himself another Chivas, nods agreement.

Your mother gets up to check that the gazpacho hasn't boiled over.

Then they tell us that Van Zyl Slabbert has resigned as leader of the opposition.

I can take a lot after 10 years of SABC TV news. I was even able to deal with the Big News of Prince Andrew's rumoured engagement (although your mother has now despaired of ever marrying off your sister Gloria to someone with a British passport). But Supervan's desertion has left me with an empty feeling gazpacho will not fill. I haven't felt this way since the rand dropped to 35c.

I stood by the party when Helen was the only MP. I ran the tombola stall at the fete at Zoo Lake year after year. I gave up a trip to Mauritius for the Slabbert Trust. It was never the Liberal Party, but then Alan Paton was never Van Zyl Slabbert. It took the party 20 years to find an ex-rugby-playing intellectual of true Afrikaans stock with no connections to Anglo American. Now they'll probably have to settle for Pik Botha.

Your uncle Harry says he's had a top tip PW's going to announce a total Cabinet reshuffle: Pik replaces Magnus, Magnus replaces Baby Doc, Baby Doc replaces Savimbi and your mother is sent to sort out the Bophuthatswana problem, on account of her extensive knowledge of Sun City.

Your grandmother had fallen asleep during a report denying the imminent release of Mandela. She wakes up to pictures of Slabbert's press conference.

"What happened? Did they release Slabbert?" she asks.

"You're right, gran," your sister retorts. "Ten years in Parliament must be like a lifetime in Pollsmoor."

The family you left behind may be a bit wearing but the Rastafarian is really something special. I'm not sure what attracts your sister to him. Is it the dreadlocks that go down to his knees? Is it the saxophone permanently draped around his neck? Is it the age-old T-shirt proclaiming, "F... art, let's rock'n'roll"? Or is it his inherent sense? While we were discussing the difference between Parliament and Pollsmoor he went off to raid your mother's spice rack for something to smoke.

Stevie, my son, do you think you could find room in your Battersea squat for an ageing ex-member of the Liberal Party who once ate at the same table with Jan Steytler?

Failing that, maybe you'll come home.

Since I know the only way to get you home is to stop the British taxpayer supporting your "studies" and your South London "accommodation", as of last night I'm in favour of Maggie's education cuts. I'm therefore writing a letter to Maggie, while she's still in office, to tell her to stop supporting London School of Economics students whose loyalty to the empire, the queen and the Tories could be called into question. I will give her your last known address.

Your loving father,

Dad

cc: 10 Downing Street.

February 14 1986

"Mon-Imali"

Linksfield

Johannesburg

My Son,

I am writing to you on my new Kumquat word processing software, called AutoGordimer. It is a unique programme, having no full stops but an abundance of commas. It is at least an improvement on my first effort, called the AutoCoetzee, which was not user-friendly, but won a lot of prizes. I might just try an AutoBrink, with a built-in translator and a two-colour screen. My real triumph, however, will be AutoRhetoric, designed specifically for press releases, public speeches and statements of policy. There is a fair demand for that sort of thing around these parts, Gloria tells me.

Anyway, my son, it has been an educative week. For example, I bet you thought the fate of the Black Sash was to see out the revolution on a Jan Smuts Avenue corner, sheltering from the bullets behind an AutoRhetoric placard.

You were wrong. But don't worry, so was I. I learnt this week that the fate of the Black Sash is all about home-baked cakes, home-made jams, home-made sandals, home-made jewellery and home-made Msinga baskets. The Black Sash fate wears a straw hat, a hand-woven jersey and sensible shoes. It happens in an Illovo garden this Saturday morning.

We have been preparing for the Black Sash fate – sorry, fête – for two weeks. Beauty has never worked so hard. She has baked, sewn, cooked, polished, shined, crocheted, knitted.

Barney has been polishing his donation: his auxiliary bazooka, two AK-47s and a rocket launcher plus 17 rounds of ammunition. He is planning to raffle them all as one unit – the Dennis Goldberg Collection.

Your mother is preparing to run a special affidavit-taking course for new recruits. All participants will get a free Rural Research Package: a pen, a clipboard, affidavit forms, a portrait of Saul Mkhize, a toothbrush, a spoon and a list of volunteer lawyers.

I will be selling Kumquats, which is why I am working on new programmes suitable to Saturday morning markets. I have a special for the Johannesburg Democratic Action Committee, called AutoCaucus. It has a unique device that rejects all commands until full consultation with the popular democratic masses has taken place.

There is a special version for the End Conscription Campaign. It is called AutoArrest. The person who switches it on is detained immediately and is held until a lawyer takes the matter to the supreme court.

The lawyer, of course, makes use of a programme called AutoInterdict. At the mere mention of the word "costs", it produces masses of paperwork, a Natal judge and a team of American-financed advocates.

The state, on the other hand, will be able to buy a special programme for informers and spies, called AutoTeller.

For the trade union movement, there is a combination of AutoSecede and AutoAmalgamate, but I fear production will be impeded by the ideologues of the Kumquat and Allied Workers Union, a breakaway from the Kumquat and General Workers Union, which bears no relation to the Federation of Kumquat Workers.

I am also producing a special for the Black Sash itself. It is called AutoAffidavit. This remarkable machine travels to unknown villages with unpronouncable names, finds with impeccable accuracy the most unfortunate residents, takes down all their relevant details, informs the press and suitable MPs and pickets the local administration board. It is entirely compatible with AutoInterdict and half-compatible with AutoCaucus.

South African Council on Sport supporters will be able to invest in AutoBoycott. Based on the principle "no normal computer in an abnormal society", it will refuse to operate until apartheid is abolished.

I couldn't leave out the journalists, of course. They will get AutoInvent, a special device that allows them to stay at home and sunbathe next to the swimming pool while the computer produces wonderful tales about events nobody cares about.

Anyway, my son, I am convinced that the only real reason for the fête is to give some people a chance to get rid of the second-hand books they bought last month at the PFP fête and others a chance to buy some books they can give back for next year's fête.

Thus is the wealth redistributed.

Your father,

Dad

October 17 1986

"Mon-Imali"
Linksfield
Johannesburg

My Son,

Crime has reared its unlovely head, bringing broken doors and marital strife to our once-peaceful suburb. I was sitting in my office last Friday, examining your latest contribution to my library - I think I prefer *Penthouse* to *Hustler*, but I'm old-fashioned – when the telephone rang. It was our next-door neighbour, Dan ("Just call me Nxongxanquaxaqua") Nyoka.

"Nx!" I said. "What's up?"

"Your dining room window, old chap," he said, "and there are one or two fellows about to climb through it."

"The family silver!" I shouted as I ran for the Merc. I was well on to the highway when I realised we haven't had any family silver since we auctioned it to pay for the first year of your LSE "studies". There is, however, the family stainless steel with plastic handles (OK Bazaars, circa 1985), the family stereo system, and the family video recorder (two).

I needn't have worried. They left everything, including a message spray-painted in day-glo pink on the wall of the lounge: "You must be kidding," it said.

Beauty had been hiding in the Nyokas' lounge, helping herself to the sherry and refusing to come back until she was guaranteed protection. Dora Nyoka was threatening to move back to Diepkloof Extension 17, where she could be safe from brazen daylight raids, although not brazen night-time raids, or to Sandton, where there was a better class of burglar. Your uncle Barney arrived half an hour later, protesting his innocence. His guilty look was due to his absence when needed – the only time, need I add, anybody has needed him since he came into our lives eight months ago.

I picked up the phone to dial the police.

"Sell-out. Informer. Collaborator," Gloria said. She was referring, I understand, to me, even though I have never been able to sell out so much as a new range of toilet seats and she always accuses me of being uninformed. "Is there something wrong with trying to prevent theft?" I asked.

"Prevent theft? You own a factory, a house, a car, two videos, you deal in shares and you feel you are in a position to prevent theft. Property is theft. What took place tonight was an attempt, sadly unsuccessful, to redistribute a little wealth. And you want to turn the culprits in."

She seemed genuinely shocked, until I reminded her that her gold-plated, quadrophonic Walkman was probably also in danger of redistribution.

Your mother, however, saw the potential for a liberal/left-wing alliance. "You can't call the police," she said, sobbing. "What if they find the culprits? They'll be arrested. And it's not their fault. They're probably suffering from the effects of Bantu education, they are unemployed and unemployable and need to steal from affluent people like us to feed their families which consist of at least 25 people, including several babies."

"But they painted on our wall," I said.

"A clear form of protest," said your mother.

I decided to call a commercial security company. If Gavin Relly is in favour of privatisation, who am I to argue?

They came out immediately and wired up all the windows. They assured us that if anybody touched the windows, a squadron of men with sirens,

Who's Left.

big boots and man-eating dogs would come immediately and protect us. Then they installed a console in a cupboard which they locked and went away with the key. Barney, showing off some of the skill he acquired during his time in detention, picked the lock.

It was a wonderful sight: a console the size of a video recorder with lights flashing – blue lights, red lights, green lights, even day-glo pink lights – and a row of buttons. I pressed one.

You may have heard the siren in Battersea. I finally threw the console across the room to stop it – but when Dan tried to go home, we couldn't open any of the doors or the windows. The house was hermetically sealed.

Or vacuum-packed.

Three hours later we heard somebody sneaking around the front garden. "Who goes there?" growled Barney, and when he got no answer, he launched a rocket – fortunately through the front door, which swung open to reveal the security company fellow lying flat on the ground behind the bougainvillea, screaming: "Take the whole house, it's yours!"

And that, my son, is something I haven't heard since shortly before the local bank manager shot himself.

Your father,

Dad

November 21 1986

"Mon-imali"
Linksfield
Johannesburg

My Son,

Last week, the Lavatory and Allied Workers Union (Lawu) decided in the interests of productivity to hold the week during the weekend and the weekend during the week in case they miss out on any long weekends once the stayaways begin.

They needed the time in any event to caucus about the buy-out. This comes as a change – they usually only talk about sell-out in my presence.

But in view of my impending disinvestment, the status of the financial rand, which is now down to eight cents and three Chappies, the high cost of containerisation to Nicaragua and the small gratuities involved in acquiring travel documents for Gloria's hangers-on – the boys in the band National Suicide – I have decided to make available to Lawu and its associates the whole bloody bang-shoot.

Basil Tshabalenskaya, our shop steward, has been on the phone ever since to his colleagues in the Lavatory Brush, Pan, Plunger and Allied Workers Union, which is a breakaway from the Urinals, Septic Tanks and Bidet Guild, trying to talk them into throwing in their lot with him. "Come on," I heard him urge on Thursday, "you have nothing to lose but your chains."

Meanwhile, every time we open a cupboard at home, it seems as though rather than disinvesting, your mother has gone in for a local takeover of Macro, Woolworths, Boardmans and all the curio shops in the Carlton Centre. She is operating on the assumption that there are no knickers in Nicaragua and that unless we stockpile enough Anchovette for our descendants, family life will fall apart. She has also decided that in order to make our allegiances plain, we will have to be garbed in Ndebele bridal aprons at all times. Since the band appropriated the first consignment, she has had to order five more gross from Beauty's cousin who has a factory in Lusaka, part of the burgeoning border industries encouraged by the new budget, the "election", the July intake and the phasing out of influx control.

Also, I keep stumbling over leather couches. They are in the bedroom, in the laundry, in the bathroom, in the fridge – not inside, on top – in the garage, hemming in the BMW, and there's even one in the jacuzzi, where your mother is trying to soften it up before departure. These couches come in a range of colours, none of which cows come in, and a number of styles, ranging from overstuffed to obscene.

You must understand that leather couches are a new way of being subversive which, as yet, is not against the emergency, although I believe a fellow called Stoffel is looking into them. It seems he can't believe people will actually find a use for, say, seven cerise couches and three turquoise two-seaters in, for example, Dallas. He has been taking a few sample sofas apart in the hope that he'll find they are being used to smuggle diamonds, dagga, ANC literature, Ndebele beadwork or, for that matter, Ndebeles.

I think Beauty is going to be a problem when it's time to board the plane. She was already raring to go, shouting "Olé!" at the slightest provocation and speaking in rhyming couplets because she had heard that to get into the government you have to be a poet.

So what happens? On Friday suddenly she finds herself the owner of 14 racehorses, a Mercedes dealership and a soccer team – and a lot of aggravation, because she already has a soccer team, you may remember, and although the stables below her condo can easily handle the 14 horses, the palace is not big enough for two lots of 11 bulky midfield defenders.

She came by the racehorses, the Mercedes dealership and the soccer team honestly, she says. She happened to be walking past the Standard Bank repro section and "they made an offer I couldn't refuse", she says. The soccer team she is minding for a friend.

Or, should I say, we are minding the team – because claiming they were driving her crazy, she lit out on Sunday for the Comrades, taking her own with, and we haven't seen her since.

Your father,
Dad

June 5 1987

Too hot to Trotsky, too young to die

Thomas Equinus

Some of the world's truly monumental events happen in call boxes.

Take the relatively recent example of Brother Horace, a Catholic priest from London with unique powers of levitation. He got his mother to knit him a jumper with a huge "S" on it (for Supersaint), slipped it on in telephone booths, and waved to unemployed West Indians as he rose recreationally to be "nearer my God to thee".

Horace died in 1976 when, in a state of religious ecstasy, he failed to spot the Concorde.

A similarly significant event involving a call box happened last week in Cape Town. A member of the Trotskyist Marxist Workers Tendency (MWT) phoned the *Mail* with a 10c piece tied to a piece of string, to report that the MWT was alive and well and preaching a pure form of revolution.

As a lifelong supporter of Lev Bronstein, all I can say is full marx to them. We Trotskyists have much to offer the world, like the strategy of "entryism".

Ever since I entered the Church I have been a proponent of entryism. After preaching it for a while I found a number of interested nuns willing to practise what I preached. The doctrine prospered for months until Sister Maria Teresa – in a peculiarly Freudian blunder – absent-mindedly put her diaphragm in the collection plate.

We Trotskyists also have many endearing insights into wage disputes. We adhere religiously to Lenin's precept that no one should be paid more than a skilled worker.

This egalitarian principle has been completely rejected in *The Daily Mail* salary structure, which looks like the financial equivalent of the Great Chain of Being. In this hierarchical, medieval system the Fat and Thin Editors emerge as Gods of Capital, with department heads levitating as angels round the divine throne of wealth.

I prop up the Great Chain of Capital as an impecunious Satan.

All because the Editors have decided to define a "skilled worker" as someone with a doctorate in linguistics and 25 years' experience in the newsroom.

We Trotskyists have, for many years, defined a skilled worker as someone able to get to the office by 9.30 in the morning.

The MWT's insistence on an armed people and no standing army is infinitely better than an armed army and no standing people, while anyone who has watched AmaZulu supporters in action will see the sense of promoting self-defence against Inkatha.

Even more than capitalism, we hate everything associated with Stalinism, like the *Daily Mail* share scheme. My personal convictions in this regard have been reinforced after reading the memoirs of WG Krivitsky. Krivitsky was an old fashioned leftwinger for Dynamo Moscow and looked set to take his place in the 1938 World Cup squad.

But he was spotted dribbling past three defenders in a league match and was accused of individualism by the selectors. From then on the OGPU (the Russian equivalent of the Johannesburg city council) watched his every move on the field and soon thereafter, when he contributed to a slow midfield build-up in a cup tie, he was accused of Fabian Gradualism and asked to come to a Molotov cocktail party thrown by Stalin.

Wisely he RSVP-ed that he had a prior appointment with a productivity committee and – disguised as a 14-year-old gymnast in a diplomatic pouch – flew to the West that night.

It is abundantly clear that the MWT is the only hope for mankind (and a couple of women) and a recent "Too Hot to Trotsky" party at the Cannes Film Festival fuels my hopes. I've never heard of this party, but if it has imperialist film stars as members I'm willing to join to influence their politics with some entryism.

June 15 1990

The day the fetish priestess came to church

Cameron Duodu

At exactly 11 minutes past 11am on August 11 Britain went bananas. An eclipse of the sun was seen in full totality in parts of the country. Cornwall and Devon were supposed to be two of those places, and great preparations were made by campsite managers and hoteliers to fleece the six million people who were expected to throng the place to see the last solar eclipse of the millennium.

But the British weather put paid to all that. The weather forecast said Cornwall and Devon would be clouded over on the day, and that it would even rain. So only a fraction of the expected hordes turned up.

Television, as usual, proved to be the best purveyor of the eclipse wonder. The BBC sent a Hercules aircraft above the clouds to photograph the event.

And it was spectacular. First it looked as if some monster in the sky was taking tiny bites out of the sun. Then the tiny bites became crescent-shaped. And finally the sun disappeared altogether.

At this point, the commentators ran out of superlative adjectives. Even Patrick Moore, the BBC man who dwells in *The Sky at Night*, was reduced to only a few words per minute, as against the 50 000 words per second with which he normally catapults his tongue into orbit.

We in London were only expecting a 95% eclipse, and indeed, my corridor darkened as the moment arrived. It really was eerie, as the darkness fell, stayed around for a while, and then made its way back where it had come from, and bright sunshine was fully restored.

It took me back to May 20 1947, when I was a tiny boy in Ghana. We had heard rumours that on that day the "sun would set" in the early afternoon, but "sunrise" would follow, not the next day, but shortly afterwards on the same day!

We knew nothing about eclipses. All we knew was that the sun rose and that the sun set. So these rumours troubled us deeply. Those who had a little knowledge of the Bible told us about darkness coming at an unscheduled hour at the time Jesus was crucified. Others mentioned Joshua and Gideon.

The more apocalyptically minded frightened us with gruesome stories from Revelations telling about the time Jesus would descend down to sentence all sinners to eternal death by burning.

Anyway, the day arrived. Its frightening aspect was heightened by a circular which the white district commissioner had sent to all the chiefs in our area, asking them to beat gong-gong to advise farmers to return home early if they went to work in the forest. We interpreted this to mean that ghosts and goblins would be about that day, and that if we went to the farm, dwarfs, elves and every frightening creature imaginable would be waiting to pounce on us. As would, of course, animals that hunted at night.

Not to be outdone, the Presbyterian church, which ran our school, ordered a special service that afternoon. Our school, which had been due to reopen on that day after the holidays, was told not to.

It was as if the fetish priests and priestesses (sangomas) had bribed the civil and church authorities to advertise their wares. All the normally insecure people who feared that witches would make medicine (muti) against them went to buy special day-of-darkness talismans to protect them from every pestilence you could think of.

Barren women were given special potions to smear on their stomachs while they made love on that day. And sexually dysfunctional males were instructed to find a secret place where they could take out their organ and expose it to the dying embers of the sun, till "daybreak". If anyone saw them doing this, they could forget about ever having an erection again.

Members of my household scorned all these things. Yet we took the precaution of gathering together at the queen mother's palace, where we knew we would have the strength of numbers. The queen mother sat with us; her officials drank palm wine and told jokes. We kids made forays into the royal kitchen to see whether we could assuage our permanent hunger.

Three o'clock – nothing. Some of the men, now ridden high by the palm wine, began to ridicule the rumours.

"How can the sun set in the daytime?" Hahahaha.

"How can the sun set and rise within the space of a few minutes?" Hahahaha.

"So when it sets in the daytime and you sleep, will you dream?" Hahahahaha.

But at about 4pm they were suddenly driven silent. The sky had began to darken. And continued to darken!

Then the weirdest thing of all happened: the chickens began to cluck. One by one, they made their way to their sleeping places.

At this stage, the queen mother got scared. She ordered: "Beat the drums!"

The kids cowered and huddled together in corners. We began to cry, louder and louder as the darkness increased in intensity.

The men brought the drums and began to beat them. I have never since heard drums beaten with such earnestness.

Over at the Presbyterian church, they began to peal the church bell. They sang a hymn: *Darkness Has Fallen upon the Earth*!

In the middle of the service, they saw the most powerful fetish priestess enter the church and take a seat. She had taken off all her usual talismans and juju beads. She remained a Christian convert to her last day.

August 13 1999

Black women can jump (reluctantly)
Angella Johnson

Me, jump out of a plane at 3 000m? You must be joking. No way! Not this side of life. I could not have emphasised the point more strongly when my editor suggested, with an evil grin, that I try skydiving for this column. I gave him one of my "you're outta your mind" slitty-eyed glares. He gave me one of those "I didn't know you were such a coward" looks. And nothing, nothing causes me to lose a grip on reality quite like a dare.

So that is how I ended up crammed with eight other lunatics into a sardine tin they call a plane (it is about the size of your average saloon car, only elongated), climbing 3 000m into the sky so that we could hurl ourselves out into the air.

I was really not ready for it. My bladder was full to bursting, I had not written a will and (this is crucial) my mind does not tolerate heights – I get dizzy just standing on a chair. No job was worth this much anguish, I told myself. It had seemed so different on land. More tranquil and graceful. Watching the brightly coloured suits of the Pretoria Skydiving Club members float in the sky like birds, I had even lost some of my overnight dread of the event.

"It's great, man. Such a rush," exclaimed 18-year-old matric student Michelle Alfredo, who had made her first jump the previous week and was back for more. "There's nothing like that feeling of adrenaline pumping through your body. You'll love it."

Such enthusiasm from one so young and the presence of a group of about 30 other skydiving enthusiasts (plus a couple of virgin jumpers like myself) lulled me into the false impression that this was indeed just a normal sport.

These people met every Saturday and Sunday and paid good money to do this. Admittedly, they were mainly adrenaline junkies – most had either bungee-jumped from the Victoria Falls bridge or done some other death-defying danger stunt at some time in their life.

Take Ted Summerlee, a long-haired, bejewelled catering co-ordinator for South African Airways. He has made about 360 jumps during the past two years. "I was looking for something exciting to do," he said enthusiastically. "This seemed like just the ticket."

Summerlee had already done speed motorbike riding, was a member of the Porsche club and had bungee-jumped several times. "I sat down and worked out that this was the next step within an affordable price bracket."

He became hooked after the first jump. "It's like when you're out there nothing can hurt you. You're just flying," he waxed lyrical. "It's even better than sex." (Now you see why I was seduced into going up.)

So much so that it did not sink in when he told me why he had not skydived for six weeks. Something to do with jumping out of a plane over Potchefstroom late one night, hitting a power line, losing consciousness, plummeting to the ground face-first and waking up in the Linksfield Clinic three days later suffering from memory loss.

Unfortunately, my memory is working just fine and all this comes rushing back to me in the airplane.

Mark Farrell, my instructor on this tandem skydive, hunkers down in front of the door looking very cool. A well-built chap (I hope the parachute can take our combined weight), he is the one wearing the parachute. I clutch his hand like a lifeline.

Derek Bauer's World

The other guys in the plane are experienced formation divers. They casually discuss technique and the various positions they plan to practise for competing in national championships.

I'm desperately trying to keep calm. Have I really paid R500 – an extra R170 gets you video coverage – to do this? One of the guys senses my fear and tries to help by pointing out the various landmarks. "Over there is the N1 motorway to Pietersburg," he says.

I glance down at the miniature landscape. It just makes me feel worse. Oh shit! I can't do this … I don't want to do this. The panic is rising in me like bile. I have that sinking feeling – a sensation akin to that of losing control of one's bowel movement.

"Ten thousand feet." Farrell's shouts over the hum of the engine bring me swiftly back to reality. "Get ready," he instructs, then slides open the door. I look out at nothing and almost lose it.

It is without a doubt the most frightening moment of my entire life. Noooo, I scream at him, I don't want to do it any more! It's my money! I've changed my mind!

It is like shouting at a brick wall.

"Put your foot out on the step," he orders. I consider what would happen if I resist and decide that as we are hooked together – his front to my back – it might actually be more dangerous than just doing it. I cross my arms, close my goggle-protected eyes and hurl myself out sideways.

For the first second or so we just fall. Then I adopt an arching position – they call it the banana – and Farrell pulls the chute open. Whoosh, we are propelled upwards with a jolting motion and the straps around my legs tighten - actually, it's bloody painful. Feels like I am supporting both of us by my inner thighs. My eyes are streaming from the air pressure, my nose is running and I'm petrified. I just want this to be over.

"Relax and enjoy it," urges Farrell.

"I don't want to enjoy it. I just want to get back to land," is my belligerent reply. I seriously want to cry with frustration, fright - and that pain from my inner thighs.

Farrell is doing his tour-guide thing – pointing out the Pretoria city skyline and the descending solo skydivers from our plane. But my mind is a blur. I blubber incoherently about people who do this being mad. Just get me down, I plead. We are falling fast yet only some three minutes (why does it seem more like three hours?) have elapsed. I start to relax a little as it dawns on me that all is going smoothly.

The ground is rushing to meet us. Oh no, landing time. I've forgotten what to do. Panic manifests itself as hysterical blood-curdling screaming. Everyone from the club rushes out to watch.

Farrell shouts instructions, but it is too late. Thud! We come down with an inelegant bump, my left foot is twisted in a strange angle. Fortunately, Farrell acts as a convenient cushion.

People surround us, helping to unhook the parachute. "How was it?" ... "Did you enjoy it?" ... "Wasn't it great?" ... "How do you feel?" I take a deep breath and opt to answer the last question. I feel as if I've just narrowly escaped a car crash. "That's the adrenaline," Farrell explains. "Some people's heart rate goes over 200." I'm surprised I didn't have a heart attack.

The whole thing had taken about 10 minutes from the moment we got into the plane – it took me a further 15 minutes to regain complete control of my faculties.

Would I do it again? No way. Not unless the aircraft was on fire and there was no other way out. I'd rather streak naked across a football pitch. I am clearly not an adrenaline junkie.

July 3 1998

In Africa, the conmen do it with style
David Beresford

With the pork-pie hat he looked like a private detective out of a Dashiel Hammett novel, but I was damned if I was going to stop for him. Then he produced his police warrant card and asked why I had given money to a known terrorist and suspected drug dealer.

It was time to stop walking and start listening.

I didn't believe he had been a terrorist. And all I had given him was 20 shillings and a cup of coffee.

But then it was Nairobi, in the aftermath of the rioting, so paranoia was understandable. And, besides, I had never forgotten being thrown into prison for a night in Zimbabwe. Or the police commander who had admonished me the next day: "But you must have done something; you're in prison, aren't you?"

I had met the "terrorist" as I had walked into the British high commission in the Kenyan capital. He had given me lots of white teeth and a big hello and made me confess that, yes, I was from Britain.

Enthusiastically he confided he was shortly going to study economics at the University of London. Could he buy me a cup of coffee in return for a run-down on the place?

I brushed him off, gesturing over my shoulder at the coat of arms and explaining I had an appointment.

But the high commission was closed. Back out I came, and was just walking into a coffee shop when he materialised again from nowhere. So, resignedly, I sat down with him and he started to spin his tale – a South African refugee ... 21-day visa had just run out ... trying to get to Djibouti ...

I saw it coming and cut him off. I did not mind buying him a cup of coffee and telling him about London, but I could not help him with money. He looked crestfallen and I felt guilty. When the change came I gave him the 20 shillings and then he cheered up and asked for my address in London

– "Then I can drop you a postcard if I make it to England" – which I scribbled on a piece of paper, wishing him good luck and goodbye.

I was heading back to my hotel when they picked me up, Pork Pie and his squad. They said they had arrested my "contact". They had seen me give him money and an address.

When had I come into the country? Did I know there were attempts to overthrow the government of Kenya? Did I want to talk, or did they have to take me to the police station? "Come, we'll sit down over there," they said, leading me to a table at a cafe on the other side of the road.

I went with them, resignedly wondering if there were rats in Kenyan jails. "You must have done something; you're in prison, aren't you?"

You could tell Pork Pie was a professional; his interrogation technique was a treat – constantly shifting the line of questioning, never allowing one to build up a coherent reply, punctuating the pauses with, "Are you going to tell the truth, or do we have to take you to the police station?" A couple more of his colleagues had joined us, including an older man I mentally dubbed "the professor".

"Do you think if we took you in front of a magistrate he would believe that?" demanded Pork Pie. "Come on, how would you bail yourself out in front of a magistrate?" He paused. "You know what bail is, don't you?" he demanded as I looked bewildered. "Bail. It's money. You pay money for bail." He sounded exasperated.

"How much?" I asked. "200 pounds," ejaculated the professor. "But you'll have to promise never to do it again," hurriedly added Pork Pie. I gazed at my feet, pondering, then looked up. "I think we have to go to the police station," I said slowly.

They stared at me. The professor had sweat on his brow. I rose to my feet and wagged a finger. "You're not cops, you're just a bunch of bloody gangsters."

I turned, bounced off an adjoining table and, trying to maintain an appearance of indignant dignity, walked off, braced for the shout that would tell me if I had it wrong – crooked cops, or conmen.

It didn't come.

It was a beauty; a two-phase sting – and in Africa. I'm no stranger to crime; few people are. Perhaps the worst on the continent is Senegal, where the gangs of pickpockets are like flies around a rotting carcass.

I still treasure the memory of a colleague from *The New York Times* running into our hotel lobby in Dakar gasping: "God, they nearly got me."

He had made the mistake of taking a stroll outside the hotel's security perimeter. "One guy went for my jacket pocket," he panted. "Then another pulled at my trouser leg. As I bent over to knock his hand away another went for my back pocket. I blocked him and just turned and ran. I don't know how I got away," he smiled. Then he grabbed his left wrist with his right hand and a look of incredulity crossed his face. "Oh God," he said. "They got my watch."

And then there is South Africa, of course. Which is just brutal. At Christmas five men with knives took my shoulder-bag in the middle of Cape Town in mid-afternoon. About a year ago a man grabbed the strap of my bag in downtown Johannesburg as I ran through a crowd of commuters. I turned. "Yes?" I said. It only dawned that he was a mugger when he started cursing at someone behind me. It still sends a chill down my back when I think of what the second man had failed to do.

Which is why I will remember Pork Pie and his men with a degree of fondness. It is nice to see a touch of style brought to crime in Africa.

July 27 1990

Who stole George Fivaz's kettle?

Angella Johnson

It would seem that not even the national police commissioner is safe from South Africa's tidal crime wave.

Thieves broke into one of George Fivaz's offices last weekend and made off with two large fax machines and a kettle.

The bold-faced crooks marched into what should be one of the country's safest buildings – police headquarters in Schoeman Street, Pretoria – and helped themselves to the equipment.

According to a spokesman for the commissioner, Joseph Ngobeni, it was not clear whether this was an inside job or not. "Someone simply walked into my secretary's office and helped themselves to the goods. There was no one working at the time and the building is usually empty over the weekend."

Ngobeni said the theft was only discovered on Monday when people arrived for work. "The police were called in and are now investigating the incident."

The fax machines were being used in the media department. Their disappearance caused a glitch in the distribution of faxes to media organisations, before they were replaced.

But the thieves will find that not all of their booty will be of use to them – the kettle was electric and in their haste they managed to leave the base behind.

This latest incident once again highlights the question of security within police buildings.

Over the years there have been numerous cases of property disappearing from police stations – the most celebrated incident being the break-in at John Vorster Square, where about R2-million was stolen from a huge safe.

It is rumoured that following his appointment as national police commissioner nearly 20 months ago, Fivaz raised the possibility of employing a private security firm to guard his offices.

The matter was quickly dropped when it became apparent that this might cause a degree of embarrassment to the department. Security was then left in the hands of the police.

August 8 1996

Gym is worse that jail
Krisjan Lemmer

Greg Blank, Africa's most famous former insider trader, felt the rough edge of justice recently. He was at the Krok brothers' Health and Racquet Club in Sandton and had his sports bag nicked. Forlornly, he made a point: he hadn't had a single thing pinched by a lower class of crook when he was the president's guest in his well-appointed suite at the Krugersdorp prison for six months.

April 18 1997

Part Two
Hot Airtime
(and other Media)

Masters in tedium
Gus Silber

On assignment for Network in Namibia last week, Cliff Saunders took time off from his hectic schedule to pay a visit to Sam Nujoma's mother. Fortunately for her, she wasn't home. Unless she was hiding in one of the scraggly huts on her humble abode which, as Cliff pointed out, was in stark contrast to the "affluence and jetsetting lifestyle which her son so readily sports in public".

Accompanied only by an entire platoon of South African reconnaissance commandos and a modest convoy of armoured cars, Cliff hopped off a Casspir, dodged a few of Sam Nujoma's mother's chickens and set off to interview the woman who had said Mrs Nujoma was not in at the moment. She helped him with his inquiries.

"Does Sam Nujoma send money to his mother?" asked Cliff, through an interpreter.

The woman shook her head. "Why doesn't Sam Nujoma send money to his mother?" persisted Cliff, wearing a spotless safari waistcoat in stark contrast to the woman's oily rags. She shrugged her shoulders.

Then Cliff climbed into one of the armoured cars which the South African Defence Force so readily sports in public, and the convoy churned up dust in its continuing quest to track down relatives of Sam Nujoma who hadn't received a cheque in the post since the declaration of independence.

For his dedication to duty and his relentless determination to uncover a new angle in the Namibian conflict, Cliff Saunders deserves to be nominated for an Artes Award in the category of Best Contribution to a Public Affairs Programme. Should this Award be the case, Cliff would be well-advised to make like Sam Nujoma's mother and not be available for the occasion. For on a sliding scale of acceptable evils, hiding away in a hut in Okandjero must surely be preferable to sporting an Artes award in public.

This theorem was proven beyond all doubt on Saturday night, when the SABC crossed over to the SABC for a live transmission of Artes '89, the moment millions of viewers had been waiting for to get up and grab some coffee before going to bed. I persevered, however, if only because Artes non-nominee Eben Engelbrecht had so tantalisingly previewed the big occasion on the *News at Eight*.

Standing in the foyer of a studio at Auckland Park, he identified important guests ("And here comes the Minister in the Office of the State President entrusted with Information, Broadcasting Services and the Film Industry, Mr Stoffel van der Merwe") and filled us in on what was going to happen in a few feverish minutes from now.

"In Studio Five, technicians are feverishly preparing for the countdown ... seating for several hundred people has been arranged on the studio floor ... those lucky enough to have been invited will witness a spectacular variety show as well as see South Africa's top television performers being awarded the sought-after Artes ..."

It sounded unmissable, especially the bit about Stoffel van der Merwe sitting on the floor. The reality is too tedious to recount, but suffice to say that Artes '89 at least solved the nagging conundrum of how exactly the SABC managed to make a net profit of R53,8-million in the last financial year.

Easy. They made the money by cutting down on the budget for Artes '89. They did away with the rainbow smoke and the girls in feathers and left us with a bunch of boys mincing mercilessly in bondage gear to canned Michael Jackson. They did away with the slick lighting and nifty camera cutaways and left us with blurred bits of vaguely famous people in the dark.

They did away with the space-age decor and left us with a giant revolving lobster claw and the kind of mock-velvet wallpaper normally found in the lavatories of renovated hotels in Boksburg.

The only thing they didn't do away with was the public transmission of the Artes Awards ceremony.

Perhaps they would like to give this some thought before next year's ceremony. Otherwise I'm going to grab myself a cup of coffee. In Okandjero.

April 28 1989

Rules for secretaries
Krisjan Lemmer

Are you thinking of becoming a secretary at the SABC? I certainly was, until I read the latest edition of *Interkom*, the SABC's internal magazine. It has an article on what is expected of a secretary – not by the boss, but by the boss's wife.

Following a talk given by Samphia Els, wife of the managing director of Dions, and Di Hood, wife of OK head Gordon, the *Interkom* editors have drawn up a little test for secretaries.

Is your perfume overwhelming? Can you resist wearing a backless dress on hot days? Do you check that your jerseys are not "too stiff"? How short is your miniskirt? Can you sit comfortably?

If you score less than 12, you need to re-examine yourself. I don't know where to start.

July 12 1991

The witch and the toad

Robert Kirby

I thought I might introduce my brand-new assignment as the *M&G's* television ruminant with a merry thought from Mr Theo Erasmus. Mr Erasmus – or Thunderbox Theo as he's known to his professional intimates – is General Manager of SABC3. According to rumour, Theo earned this moniker from his habit of going all frothy around the colon when anything disagrees with him.

Example: a paragraph from a crumpled letter Thunderbox sent to the Broadcasting Complaints Commission, griping about my continued presence on that morally patient body. Hyperbole firmly clenched in his teeth, Thunderbox wrote:

"We concede that the readers of a publication such as the *Financial Mail* may discount such vitriolic attacks on this channel and the SABC as the smug subjectivity of poison-pen journalism and that some might even be vaguely amused by it. However we are concerned about the effect this has on our staff; on creative people doing a splendid job. Such unjustifiably acrimonious, destructive criticism has a demoralising effect, which can only be to the detriment of the SABC and the South African television industry as a whole."

And there you were, thinking humble television critics are naught but chaff in a gale. You were wrong. With a twitch of our toxic keyboards we are capable of demoralising entire industries. Never undervalue us.

Introductions over, let me move on and take a look at the newest labour of one of the SABC's most talented curiosities, Mr Phil Molefe, an editor-in-chief in the SABC news department. When he's not busy expelling colonialist debris like Max du Preez, Phil gets his creative rocks off doing impersonations of how Idi Amin would have looked as a television interviewer.

Phil reserves this persona for the really important stuff. In fact the last time I saw him was earlier this year, when he and that gifted weepie, Antjie Krog, had one last desperate public lick at Mr Mandela. Last Sunday, in his latest appearance, Phil conducted a quite wonderfully bizarre long-distance interview with Libya's Colonel Gadaffi which, if nothing else, showed just how far the well-practised tongue can stretch. The encounter went on for well over half an hour, interrupted every 10 minutes by the duty newsreader whose task it was to apologise for the poor sound and reassure us that we were still tuned in to the SABC.

Indeed, we might well have wondered. At one end was Phil Molefe slowly reading a set of guzzle-arse questions ("And now, Colonel Gadaffi, please tell us how you so nobly undertook the mammoth task of keeping prices of tea and bread down for the millions of your gratefully adoring people who for so long have suffered under the criminal sanctions of the American money-gods?"), on the other, the lovable dusty colonel, looking like he'd just been thrown off a *Star Wars* set.

Abandoning his home tent for this interview, Gadaffi had elected to sit in front of some shelves of impressive-looking books, impatiently drumming his fingers on the desk while Phil drooled on. To every three words the colonel uttered in response, his interpreter added another three hundred from a nearby echo-chamber. The net result was a sort of ponderous idiot's burlesque, some Samuel Beckett reject about metaphrastic political teleology. Nay, I make perhaps too much of this. It was probably just constipation.

There you are, Theo. Let's hope the above unsolicited encomia will cast our tortured relationship adrift on more amiable waters. As the witch said to the toad, dropping him into the cauldron, "You're probably tastier boiled than baked."

September 3 1999

Good morning. Here is our Sunday freakshow
Arthur Goldstuck

One Sunday morning Radio South Africa played a snatch of Spike Milligan reading a list of "auction items" in a tired, old voice. He went on and on, reading off objects like "One cutglass Delft decanter with extra string, two volumes on how to wean vultures, one volume on keeping well away from vultures, one early X-ray photograph of Florence Nightingale's teeth, facing east, one child's hangman's kit, one throat mallet, one uncle-frightener ...

It sounded like the usual schedule for an SABC Sunday morning.

Last week we had an expert on flower-arranging telling some of her more exciting experiences; a 67-year-old woman described how she had just earned a PhD in law of the sea; the SA Air Force's director of personnel procurement stated that national servicemen should feel "proud and privileged" to be soldiers; an antique dealer described his personal collection of musical instruments, which included an 1880s German guitar lute and copies of a defunct *Banjo Mandolin Guitar Magazine*.

To cap it all, a Scottish missionary blithely told us that his grandfather had been a feared head-hunter with a superb collection of heads outside his hut in a remote Indian village. The venerable old man was teaching his son the tricks of the trade when a missionary arrived and converted our Scottish friend's father to Christianity. The fellow promptly set out into the world as a soul-hunter, and he passed this passion on to his son. Today his son uses the *Yellow Pages* to reach out to people.

You get the picture? Sunday morning on SABC is nothing less than an elaborate ecumenical freakshow. Spike Milligan would have felt proud and privileged if he had drawn up the schedule himself.

But don't be misled. This weird and wonderful carnival is no mere comedy of oddities. It has more sinister undertones.

Like Milligan's auction list, the strange guests are introduced with bland understatement. They tell their story in the faintly bored tearoom tones you'd expect to be reserved for those travel monologues that once dominated Sunday morning radio. Or they read the words from scripts with about the same depth of emotion that goes into boiling eggs.

The true intention of this somnambulent presentation can now be revealed.

Sunday morning radio broadcasters are under strict instructions not to disturb the equanimity of their listeners. Sunday, you see, is a day of rest not only for the body, but also for the mind. Uncle-frighteners aside, it is a day for avoiding anything that may raise the blood pressure.

Consider what happens when you wake up and switch on the radio. Since Sunday morning follows so closely on Saturday night, the awakening is not expected to be before about 9am, and even that is optimistic.

So there you are, waiting for your brain to engage first gear, and what your ears are feeding you is a short story about a seal which becomes stranded in a Cape Town dry dock when the sluice gates are opened. By the time the seal has made its escape 15 radio minutes later, your brain has turned off the ignition.

Then comes Simon Swindell's selection of "warm, comforting and uplifting" music, *From the Bell Tower*. Your brain is so comforted, it doesn't bother to raise you from the dead. Nothing raises you until halfway through the *Morning Service*, this week relayed live from the Assumption Catholic church, Durban.

The Reverend Pat Sammon reads from his script: "To prepare ourselves to celebrate the sacred mysteries, let us call to mind our sins."

Your brain switches on, engages reverse gear and throws you off your bed. Your sins are manifold and by the time you've run through them, it's time for *Sixty Plus*, a "programme for older listeners".

The programme order brings to mind the old joke about a kid watching his granny read the Bible. He reasons: "She's cramming for her finals." But your brain has heard the joke a few times too many and it has no interest in sexagenarianist programming.

So it idles along in neutral until the news headlines at 11am, when it suddenly tries to engage sixth gear: Nine people have died in three road accidents in Natal, two have been killed in "unrest" incidents, crime in America has risen to its highest level in 20 years, Martina Navratilova won't play singles for the Yanks in the Federation Cup.

Fortunately you don't have a sixth gear in your brain, and fortunately this is just the storm before the calm.

Those sly buggers at the SABC know what they're doing.

Next we have *Sunday at Home*, which provides the direct clue to what the Sunday morning format is all about.

It is an insidious plot to keep the idle non-churchgoing masses in their homes – and thus off the streets – using subliminal hypnosis under the guise of interesting guests.

By dulling the brain and keeping the body in bed, the government ensures that you avoid the temptation to contravene the Sunday Observance Act.

If you listen to Radio 5 or 702, you're a lost cause anyway and certain to corrupt your soul at dens of sin like Jameson's or Orlando Stadium or Johannesburg Planetarium. As far as the authorities are concerned, it's your life and you can ruin it if you wish.

But if you still listen to Radio South Africa, they regard you as one of theirs – a soul that can still be saved for the Party – and they don't want you stepping out of line.

So you'll be forgiven your Saturday nights, but, once you've recovered, you may not want to forgive them their Sunday mornings.

August 7 1987

Fear and loathing in Standerton

Charlotte Bauer

Some things never change – take Des and Dawn Lindberg; take a town called Standerton. After a performing career spanning a quarter of a century, husband-and-wife team Des and Dawn are still in pretty good shape as we could see from their *Musical Scrapbook* retrospective screened by TV1 this week. It was, however, harder to tell what kind of shape the rustic Transvaal mining town of Standerton is in.

Six months after the scrapping of the Group Areas Act, *Agenda* decided to find out how whites in the Conservative Party-run town were coping with the fact of black neighbours.

The short answer is: not very well. The down-home whites of Kenitex suburbia aren't smug anymore – they're terrified, terrified that their squatting bungalows and their wire-mesh fences and their yards that look like parking lots will be overrun by primitives who wouldn't know astroturf from a fluffy dashboard cover.

Their fear and loathing has led them to adopt terror tactics, like lobbing rocks through the windows of houses newly occupied by black families with messages written on them. These messages are generally brief and to the point: "Move Soon" they say, or, "Go Back To Sakhile".

Even the mayor, a CP man called Ian Thorn, is upset about the black neighbours he has recently required. Being an official, his official response to the situation is: "We don't like it, but we have to abide by the law – for the time being ..." However, says the mayor, regaining some of his strength, "if they start a squatter camp in their backyard the municipality will immediately do something about it".

And one is left in no doubt that they would. Standerton Town Council has probably thought deeply about the problem and decided that it is only a matter of time before one of their black neighbours tries to rent out a chicken run to a family of 12 – and then they'll show those uppity kaffirs who's boss.

Funnily enough, one man who has braved the storm and moved his family into white Standerton says it's been a doddle. "In the township you can get killed. You can get your house burnt down. Whites will usually only show their dislike by signs – throwing dead dogs in your yard, and smashing windows," says Linda Shabalala, who never expected anyone to bring round a fruit cake on moving day. With a positive attitude like that, Shabalala will probably collect the stones thrown through his window and make a rockery.

"I suppose I wouldn't mind living next door to one," commented a British immigrant who seemed to have found her spiritual home in Standerton. "As long as they behave like normal people should behave."

How should normal people behave? By Standerton standards which, naturally, must be kept up, blacks will assimilate into the white community as soon as they have learned how to toss a dead dog into their neighbours' garden without getting caught.

It's hard to catch out Des and Dawn Lindberg. Filled as they are with good ideas, good works and good business sense, they are really quite shameless about trumpeting their achievements. In this hour-long programme about themselves, by themselves, for all of us, the happy, loving minstrel couple led us through 25 years' worth of stunning successes, brave censorship battles and remarkable romance. The success and enduring popularity of the Lindbergs is obvious to anyone whose ever heard of them (and, let's face it, everyone, love them or loathe them, has). But having to listen to them going on and on and on about how wonderful they are is about as interesting as watching someone knit a scarf.

Introducing their "celebration of 25 years in the business", from the front doorstep of their magnificent house in Houghton, Des snuggled up to Dawn and chuckled: "I guess this makes us the durable Des and Dawn." I guess a tin of Gant's tomato soup is durable too.

November 22 1991

It's a tough choice – jol or duty

Thami Mkhwanazi

Modern-day scribes have occupational hazards in addition to the main one, which is state repression.

It would appear that the most common problem that besets newsmen and women covering the arts these days is a conflict between joll and duty. This crop of journalists is often saddled with the problem of avoiding or limiting the consumption of alcoholic beverages provided during working hours by companies promoting records and music concerts.

The launching of records and music festivals has become an in-thing during the lunch hour these days, with deadlines often requiring entertainment reporters to file copy immediately afterwards. This can be a hassle, leading these newshounds to choose between jolling and attention to duty.

I have witnessed a number of joll-and-duty shindigs in the past three weeks, when a series of music festivals were launched at lunchtime.

Two weeks ago the Music in Marketing company launched the Radio Zulu-Maize Generation music festival at Dephon Records, which is housed on the 22nd floor in the Kine Centre. The festival took place last Sunday at Durban's King's Park stadium.

On Wednesday the same company staged a similar event at Soccer City. The occasion launched the first leg of a series of seven countrywide Telefunken-Star Music festivals. The series will kick off with the Radio Metro music festival to be held at Soccer City on December 17. It will be the first such event at the multimillion-rand stadium.

Fans will have the opportunity to see their heroes live, belting out disco, gospel, mbaqanga and pop. The festival will feature such artists as Sankomota, Lucky Dube, Mercy Phakela, William Mthethwa, Chicco, Soul Brothers and Pat Shange.

I was among a host of joll-and-duty scribes and other entertainment personalities, including members of the Transvaal Cultural Desk, who were

Dr. Jack

invited to the Wednesday launch. We ascended the stairway leading to the luxurious Soccer City press suite.

A number of newsmen were already leaning over the oak-finished bar counter and sipping orange juice for a start when we entered the suite at noon.

Barman Ernest Schroeder was busy unpacking liquor and drinking glasses from cartons and displaying them for service.

The SABC TV crew were busy adjusting their cameras and lights for the event, with electric cord criss-crossing the mustard carpet. Men and women milled around the spacious suite occasionally looking at themselves in two beams finished with mirror from top to bottom. A row of soft lights hidden on the wall added to the cool atmosphere enhanced by a breeze blowing from the grandstand outside.

Three caterers stood at the ready behind the portable kitchen from which bread rolls, pap, boerewors and steak was to be served with baked potatoes and salads.

Music in Marketing MD Alan Prentice buttoned his jacket and told us: "Please do help yourselves to meals and drinks until we begin."

So we queued for food, and later we queued for coke, juice – and whisky, brandy, vodka and gin.

The noise grew and Prentice re-appeared. Behind him in a row stood cartons containing the music prizes to be given away during the festivals. The noise grew even louder as the scribes walked to and from the bar counter with doses of the happy waters. "I'm late, I must go," said one waiter, but the rest carried on.

At the end of the formalities journalists were invited to view a sample of bridges to be erected so that fans could walk freely to the pitch on December 17. Newsmen ignored this item and crammed around the bar. It was a long time before I saw cars pulling out of the stadium with loud screeches. Duty had called at last.

December 14 1989

Pass me the grater, granny dear

Melinda Silverman

I've conducted a scientific experiment over the past few months which has proved that a plastic Bic ballpoint is worth more than any flashy 486 VGA whatsit.

The unwitting subject of my experiments has been my husband, who happens to own not just one computer, but two, and a colour printer nogal, plus various other odd contraptions that spill wires all over the floor.

I have discovered that if, for example, we both have to write a handful of letters one night, I'll have finished all of them in half an hour and he'll still be faffing about trying to figure out where something called a printer driver has driven off to.

In the time it takes me to curl up in bed with an Ariston pad and a pen, and to tell Dotsie in New York about the s-k-a-n-d-a-a-l at Miriam's wedding, to tell Gisele in Atlanta about her cousin who almost made the ANC list (her poor mother should only know), not to mention Ricky in Shropshire about how the kids just loved the dolls she sent for their birthdays, my husband will have reached the Dear Sir with Reference To part ...

So I say to him: "What's the problem, hey?" and he says: "I'm busy working on a macro to automatically fill details into each letter. It's brilliant! When I'm finished, this will fill in today's date, key in the correct address, check spelling errors, print pages in reverse order and save hours of time."

And what's a macro? "Just watch this," he says. He thumps a few keys. The letter dances around the screen, then there's a kind of "blip" and it seems to vanish into a void. There's a silence. "Gosh," I say politely, "that's very clever."

"What do you mean, clever? The *&%$ system's crashed."

I'm still wondering what a macro is.

One day I needed to write a letter to the bank, one of those cold and nasty missives one resorts to when yelling over the phone no longer works.

I thought: "This needs to be done on a computer. Only a computer can produce letters suitably chilling and impersonal." So I scribbled down the contents (it was only about two paragraphs) and handed it to my resident computer boffin to "knock off" (his words, not mine) on his 48 something whatsit.

An hour later, I noticed that he had failed to come to bed. I stomped over to the study. He was busy on the umpteenth reprint of my letter, having designed a special rainbow-hued logo for me, having fiddled with a trillion different typestyles and margin widths and colours.

"Forget the bloody logo," I said, "just print out the letter, dash off an envelope and come to bed." Envelope? He looked astonished. Envelopes are quite tricky, he whined. First we'll have to reset this thingy and then we'll have to boot out this doodah and next we'll have to download this offload ...

I have come to understand the problem with computers. The smarter they get, the more useless they are. Word processors? They're like food processors. When you've finished grating a carrot, you have to disassemble the machine, wash five convoluted bits of plastic, and then haul out the manual to reassemble the apparatus. In the good old days, my granny just rinsed her grater under the tap.

I can think of three reasons that make word processing a bad idea:

- When you write a letter by hand, you write it once only. Word processors allow you to delete and move around and polish. And dither. A written letter is at least spontaneous.
- My husband always seems to be "configuring the system". It's a bit like a car nut who's always pulling the engine out instead of just driving the thing. "Configuring" sounds like work to him, but it sounds like play to me.
- Ever heard of a Bic pen "crashing" and losing a whole night's work? Oh yes ... that envelope for the bank manager. I wrote it out by hand.

PC Review, February 1994

Cyber-chivalry for the honourable e-mailer

Irwin Manoim

In the days when people wrote letters on sheets of paper, using instruments called pens, there were certain conventions. One was that the author wrote in full sentences ending with punctuation marks. Another was that spelling errors were avoided, lest they be interpreted as a sign of ill-breeding.

No longer. Electronic mail has seized the cursors of the masses. Full sentences, correct spelling, the occasional punctuation mark, even courtesies such as a "Dear Aunt Mathilda" at the beginning, are no longer required. Electronic mail is the literary equivalent of a grunt. Every moment of every day, waves of useless chatter rush down copper wires, cross ocean floors, sweep the globe, bounce off satellites, and dissipate into outer space. In a million years, the collected gossip of 20th-century personkind will envelop the alien inhabitants of a distant galaxy in electronic smog.

One-third of the e-mails you are likely to receive in your lifetime will be the bumbling, incoherent efforts of your friends, relatives and colleagues. The other two-thirds will be the bumbling, incoherent efforts of people you have never met, and wish never to meet, but who seem somehow to have found you, and become rather fond of you:

"Dear Sir, I found your e-mail address on the Internet. Could you please look up the address of a friend of ours whom we met on a boat trip last year, and whom we think lives in Nairobi ..."

"Hi there. Our class in Little Falls, Wisconsin, is doing a project for tomorrow on Africa. Please send all the info. Miss Flowers our teacher says very urgent ..."

"Dear Wise Investor. Would you like to earn a million dollars without doing any work? John Smith of Idaho amazed his friends when last year he answered an advert on the Internet and sent in only $50 to ..."

The electronic mail crisis has not escaped the notice of the ever-vigilant psychology profession. Occupational psychologist Professor Cary Cooper of the University of Manchester announced last week, after intensive study, that e-mails and voice-mail messages pose a health hazard. "Many people feel they have to sit at their desks to sort it all out. They have lunch at their terminals. They stop going out so much, and when they do they find they are being harassed by their pagers and mobile phones. They no longer meet people and make contacts because they feel they can't afford the time.

Dr. Jack

They become more and more aggressive towards, and intolerant of, intrusions. Stress builds up, they smoke and drink more and they suffer immune problems, such as colds, headaches and aches and pains."

If the professor is right, why do millions of apparently normal, God-fearing people opt to use e-mail? For the same reason they drive dangerous, carbon-spewing motor cars, or converse on earlobe-frying cellphones or watch mind-numbing television, or eat cholesterol-soaked food. They have to. Their friends all do it. If your friends all have e-mail, your colleagues all have e-mail, your business contacts all have e-mail, what chance do you have without it? There comes a point in your life when you gaze with shame at your e-mail-bereft business card and say to yourself: "I'd better get an e-mail address before people start sniggering at me from behind their palmtops. Without e-mail, I'm a nobody. A nobody who cannot be contacted at all hours by total strangers, former high school friends I'd rather never see again, and prostitutes in Manila offering me a good time."

E-mail will change your personality. Within a week or two you will have become a tetchy, misanthropic curmudgeon. Even if you haven't, you should try to pretend to be one, because being unpleasant is part of e-mail's charm.

How very sad, you ought to be saying by now. Is there nothing we can do to stem the ghastly tide? Why, yes, there is. After all, we live in the age of positive thinking. If each of us makes a private vow to observe a code of cyber-chivalry, we might yet salvage the last remnants of 20th-century civilisation. Here are my suggestions for a code of conduct for the honourable e-mailer.

First, please don't send me any more petitions on behalf of oppressed Afghanistan women, Serbian victims of US imperialism, Eritreans, Kurds, Tamils, Cypriots, Palestinians, US gun owners. These are probably all very nice people, but spending several hours a day solving the world's problems can knock hell out of one's diary.

If you insist on sending me an e-mail, please remember to put your name on the end, ideally the name your mother gave you. I am frequently accosted by faceless, sexless beings with names like 437855@aol.com.

When you set up your e-mail the first time round, check three times that you've filled in the "reply" field with your address correctly spelled. Plenty of people spend their lives in therapy wondering why nobody ever replies to their e-mails.

Try to send an e-mail just once. Insecure beginners habitually send the same e-mail a dozen times in the belief that, statistically, one of them ought to arrive.

Write a sensible headline in the subject field. That way, people like myself who get several hundred e-mails a day will feel a momentary pang of conscience before deleting your letter without reading it.

E-mail is more reliable than the Post Office, which is the single best reason to use it. But it can and does go astray. If you receive an e-mail from someone you know, acknowledge receipt immediately, even if you are still pondering a full response. That way the sender will know you are merely slow-thinking, rather than dead, or missing, or sulking.

Here are a few of my pet hates. Make sure they become your pet hates too. Don't write in all-capitals. One ought to feel pity for people who can't type, but do they need to pen their e-mails in all-capitals SO THAT THEY SEEM TO SHOUT LIKE THIS? Worse still are those who write entirely in unpunctuated lower case like Woodstock-era love poems.

Don't format. Old-fashioned e-mail (that is, circa two years ago) was plain text with no formatting. Along came the Microsoft oligopoly offering the opportunity to create multi-hued e-mail in every conceivable headline size and type style. Resist the temptation. Formatted e-mail takes a lot longer to download and it's the recipient who pays the phone charges. And decent people who use older, non-Microsoft e-mail programmes will see nothing but gobbledygook coding.

Avoid attachments. Attachments are separate documents, "pinned" to your e-mail. They take longer to download, require more effort to read and could contain viruses. Never send an attachment if you have a message that could just as easily be written in the body of the e-mail.

Don't send lists of names. The marvel of e-mail is that you can send the same e-mail to a hundred or so of your closest friends, with a single click. Your friends, however, may be less ecstatic if your e-mail arrives topped off with the addresses of everyone else on your list. Some of them may enjoy snooping around in your personal address lists, particularly if they can spot a few secret lovers. The rest may harbour deep-felt grudges after scrolling past reams of verbiage before reaching a one-line message like, "Hi everybody. This is just to tell you that I will be going to Plet for a week."

Here's the secret to discreet e-mailing. One of the strange fields at the top of your e-mail is marked BCC. The more curious among you may often have wondered what this might mean, since no e-mail program ever explains it. BCC stands for "blind copy" which means that if you put addresses in it, they are hidden from other recipients.

If it's big, say please. Do you have a whopper of a long document to e-mail? Or a whopper of a big picture? Ask permission first. A monstrous e-mail will not only cost the recipient a fortune in phone charges, it could also "bomb" that person's mailbox.

Don't send Microsoft Word documents. Only send Microsoft Word documents to people who live close enough to retaliate physically. Microsoft Word documents are notorious agents of Internet-borne viruses. Prudent e-mail celibates such as myself stay alive by enforcing a simple rule: we never open Microsoft Word documents that come in the mail, not even from our best friends.

Don't send WordPerfect 5 documents. Just because you haven't upgraded your computer for 11 years is no reason to expect that the rest of the world is equally tardy. Most latter-day word processors choke on ancient WordPerfect documents. Ditto for WordStar, Ami Pro and MacWrite documents. You're more than welcome to promote fringe minorities; just make sure that you figure out how to save your documents in text format.

Don't send a business card. Another Microsoft e-mailing annoyance is the opportunity to send a digital business card. It's not life-threatening, but it's as useful as computerised pizza.

Say thanks now and then. Over the years I have explained via e-mail to hundreds of American children that Johannesburg is not a suburb of Nairobi, that tigers do not roam the jungles of Gauteng, that Nelson Mandela is unavailable for one-to-one e-mail chats. I have looked up phone numbers in the Jo'burg phone directory on behalf of total strangers, and I have cut and pasted the complete wording of the national anthem.

It is fortunate that no one has ever thanked me, because the day someone finally does, I shall lapse into the kind of seizure that Professor Carey warns can come of excessive e-mail use.

PC Review, July 1999

All the fouls of the air
Robert Kirby

Whether e.tv is going to survive is, of course, anybody's guess. A lot of people think it should, usually on the grounds that e.tv is a necessary evil, an independent entity against which the SABC and M-Net may be assessed.

This is nonsense. The one thing SABC television has never lacked is its native ability to be bad all on its own. It needs no lessons on how to look and sound fifth-rate. It's like one of those self-lubricating boils you used to get on your neck soon after puberty set in. You didn't need to compare it with those adorning your schoolmates. It was yuggie and humiliating all by itself.

As for M-net, well no one with a nominally serious mind could believe that e.tv represents any danger whatsoever to them. The real truth is that e.tv, the SABC and M-Net are actually in cahoots. Each one is a distinct electronic stage in the autumnal life-cycle of low-grade American television programmes. As they reach their mid-20s, a great many of these programme organisms migrate to South African television stations.

All those cruelly weathered circa 1975 sitcoms, soapies, cop series, human interest dramas, game shows first wither on the M-Net vine. Then they move on to the SABC where, according to how frail and sickly they are, they get apportioned to the various channels. After that they all limp off to e.tv to die in shame.

The only real threat e.tv poses, therefore, is territorial. This is because, since the mid-1970s, the SABC has carefully been building up a shit-for-brains audience base. It's been a frontal 25-year dumbing-down process and has succeeded in creating a great, happily grinning wedge of the population, each member of it wielding what American social psychologists call "a common trailer-park mentality". Apparently you don't have to actually live in a trailer-park to acquire a common trailer-park mentality. It's an entirely abstract blessing. Just pay your television licence fee regularly and a CTPM will grow on you automatically. Just like the boils did.

Thanks almost entirely to the SABC – though some credit should rightfully be given to Independent Newspapers – South Africa now has a devoutly stupid but otherwise commercially exploitable bottom-end social stratum, wide open for market invasion. It is these limp-brained millions which e.tv now regards with envy. Quite rightly the SABC deeply fears and resents this, which is why they currently are going full out to degrade their audience even further.

But that's the subject of a future column. For the rest of this one I want to stick to e.tv. While it's pretty clear e.tv buy their programmes by the kilo – like those bookshops where they weigh your purchases – this provides no acceptable alibi for the abysmal level of the "local content" on the e.tv roster.

Have a look at just one of e.tv's home-grown late-evening specials. It's called *Mainly for Men*, a show which once and for all explodes the myth that "real" men have any interests outside 4X4s, hangover remedies and enormous flabby tits. To service the latter infatuation this e.tv programme recently went all hugger-mugger with *Hustler* magazine, plundering Joe Theron's archives for a selection of terrifying 18-pounders. How classy can they get?

Another local gem is e.tv news, principally a forum for items about bottled three-headed Vietnamese foetuses, loving investigations of pools of blood, updates from the urogenital front – e.tv news should be subtitled *All the Fouls of the Air.* These news bulletins are often read by a fellow called San Reddy. I'm quite sure Mr Reddy is a pleasant enough chap, but something very urgently needs to be done about his elocution. He sounds as if he's publicly test-driving a new and imaginative form of spoken English in which all unnecessary vowels and consonants are left out.

The sentence "In a function in the Parliament buildings President Mbeki spoke in honour of Oliver Tambo's great political contributions" comes out via Reddy as "Inner fuck-shin parmt blings Pren Becky poke nonner Ovamvbos grey tick ablutions." Someone should tell San either to speak slower or go and get his tongue pumped up. He's setting a terrible example to the young.

For the moment that about wraps up these pleasant reflections on our new free-to-air channel. See you in *Tabloid.*

September 23 1999

Eating it up
Ferial Haffajee

Whichever way you look at it, the Africa Café's print ads are destined to get into people's nose hairs. Art director Ivan Johnson and copywriter Kyle Cockerane had designs on the "politically incorrect and cheeky" with their series of ads.

The ad which has raised the most hackles is one which reads: "We still serve white people." And no, it doesn't affirm the café's sympathy for folk of a fairer hue in the face of the Employment Equity Bill, but aims to turn a cliche on its head. "It's about Africa and cannibalism," they say.

The double meaning raised a few complaints, but most patrons have seen the joke.

Other ads in the series include those which read: "See South Africa's amazing wildlife. Then eat them" and "Our menu? Basically anything that can't run faster than our chef."

The café's budget is small, but their chutzpah is big and, like Nando's, they give their ad agency carte blanche. This seems to have paid off: in a generally quiet season, Africa Café reports good crowds.

February 20 1998

Sheep on drugs
Rant Boy

It's not just the ads that piss Rant Boy off, you know – it's the people behind them. The marketeers – sales folk who spend their lives dreaming up lies, and then getting uptight if you won't believe them. Rant Boy encountered such an instance last week at work. The magazine that Rant Boy writes for did a small feature last month – nothing hectic, just a little tongue-in-cheek piece about alternative methods of opening beer bottles. You know: "Now that so many good beers are being imported, most without twist-off caps, you might find yourself stranded without an opener. Here's how you use the security fence as a substitute" – that sort of light-hearted fluff.

Trouble is, the photographer went and used a local brand to illustrate the feature. I won't name names (we've had threats of reduced ad-spend already), so let's just use "Ratpiss" as a convenient nom-de-booze. It seems the Ratpiss representatives are annoyed because they feel the feature was common and trashy, and Ratpiss is, after all, marketed as a "sophisticated" beer.

Sure thing, guys. "Sophisticated". That's the first thing that springs to mind when you think of beer, isn't it – "sophisticated". Have you seen how sophisticated people get after 12 beers? Rant Boy's been at weddings where the guys get so sophisticated, the noise of the brawl in the car park is only drowned out by the music of teenaged kotching, or the *dronk-verdriet* wailing of the bride's mother. Some of Rant Boy's longest nights have been spent in the company of sophisticated beer-drinkers, courteous crack-addicts and energetic dagga-smokers (all of whom worked for military intelligence in a Christian democracy ... is Rant Boy making his point yet?).

If beer's so damn sophisticated, why do you have to learn to like it? You all remember the first time you tried to drink beer – it was horrible! It's definitely not something your palate craves simply for taste's sake. No, you teach yourself to drink beer for one reason – the way it makes you feel. Why do you think Esprit was invented? That's right, so kids could learn to drink! The only "sophistication" that beer ever brings to your life is the refinement of your survival instinct, so when you stagger home from the matric dance you manage to stay upright and coherent long enough to convince your parents you're not smashed.

So there you go, folks – another reason to rant against advertisers: they take themselves so damned seriously. If Rant Boy could be allowed to quote *Ab Fab*'s Edina Monsoon, he'd like to remind the Ratpiss marketeer: "You're only a drug-dealer, you know ... you can drop the attitude."

February 22 2000

Madam & Eve

Part Three
The Body Electric

Why hares should leave elephants alone
Thomas Equinus

Kama Sutra readers know that all people are divided into categories according to the size of their lingams and yonis. Tiny women are called deer, the middling ones are mares and the cavernous ones are elephants.

A man endowed with five inches of passion is a hare, the next size up is a bull and the well-hung individual is a horse. It would be indelicate of me to tell you which category I belong to; suffice to say that they don't call me Thomas the Equine for nothing.

This above-mentioned holy work on love-making suggests that people of the same proportions should stick together, mainly to spare hares the embarrassment of fresh-air shots inside an elephant.

Of course, the importance of size difference can be greatly over-estimated and this is one of the issues being discussed at the world's first conference on orgasm, currently being held on 170 stained mattresses in New Delhi. The conference has been organised by (very) prominent Indian sexologist Prakash Kothari. Kothari has long been championing pleasure without procreation in downtown Delhi so that he can get back his parking space underneath his flat.

Kothari's co-organiser is Buddy Naidoo, an expert on *Kama Sutra* love positions. He is, for example, the finest practitioner of position 54, a double reverse lotus bind which – in 1975 – brought his date six crushed vertebrae and Naidoo a charge of attempted murder.

He then underwent 12 years of therapy because of his horror of being a hare. This period he explores in his paper *The Sliding Scale of Love* – a self-pitying treatise on his failure to satisfy anyone since a pygmy from Borneo in 1963. The dissertation was met with scholarly understanding, empathy and 20 minutes of uninterrupted laughter.

This spirit of confession prevailed for three days and a number of elephant-women admitted to never having had an orgasm, although one had once felt a brief tingle when stimulated with a bookmark which had been inside *The Woman's Room*.

The mood then shifted and Fatima Govinder, author of the famous erotic novella *He's Inside, He's on Top*, questioned whether males could have multiple orgasms.

"Why do you ask?" queried the discredited Naidoo, now the only person in his row in the auditorium.

"Because my husband's a well-known fakir," she replied trenchantly.

Discussion turned to premature ejaculation when Sunil Naidoo – Buddy's younger brother – was spotted leaving the hall on 65 separate occasions during a paper entitled *Desultory Erections and the Text* by Professor Lakshmi Gavaskar from the department of applied foreplay in Punjab.

Her argument that random lisping was a powerful aphrodisiac excited a number of scholars who begged: "Pleeth come up to my room after dinner – I want to dithcuth thith further."

The final session this week will revolve around the possibility of two people achieving simultaneous orgasm. Such an occurrence was reported as recently as 1954 in Greenland, and scientists believe it could happen again before the turn of the century. The secret to synchronised excitement is, of course, to retard the male's orgasm by approximately half an hour while escalating the woman's excitement by talking dirty and looking for her clitoris with a sonar.

If the *Kama Sutra* is to be believed, mutual pleasure is a mystical experience of marvellous proportion and well worth striving for. My Catholic girlfriend and I once got within two-and-a-half minutes of it, and were much the richer for the insight it gave us into the possibilities of narrowing the gap even further.

As per usual this learned masterpiece has been subbed by the Thin Editor, a man for whom this topic is extremely important.

He has, after all, intrepidly undertaken to satisfy the same person for the next 30 years by getting married. After he'd glanced through the *Kama Sutra* dimensional categories he blushed and said to me: "This Thin Editor bit, Equinus. It's not what you think."

He then whinnied for a few minutes and put a sugar lump in his coffee.

February 15 1991

Mr Scants – the contest for all shapes and sizes
Julia Beffon

When I arrived at the Dungeon a few Friday nights ago, I had no idea I was to be a judge in the Mr Scants competition.

Just before the competition started I was approached by the organisers and, despite all protestations that I was eminently unqualified to judge such a competition, I was soon signing my name in the judges' book.

VIP guests are seated in a railed-off area near the dance floor, directly beneath the DJ's booth – an area commonly known as "the cage". Drinks, served by a very heavy-handed and charming young man, arrived. After two whiskies my mother could have been Mr Scants.

The club's dance floor was crowded. Some boogied wildly (fantasies of showbiz?), others smooched. Then the disco music gave way to sakkie sakkie; the dance floor emptied and immediately filled again with couples grooving to the rhythms of the vastrap. Later the disco came back, but it was interrupted by a request for more contestants for the Mr Scants competition, who were presumably found.

A "judging sheet" was thrust into my hands – a formal printed document listing the contestants' names (first name only), and divided into sections: poise, sex appeal, appearance, personality and crowd response. All I had to do, they assured me, was to fill in a score of one to 10 under each of these categories for each contestant, then total them up.

After that, in consultation with the other two judges, we would whittle down the 13 contestants to a preliminary seven, then after that we would

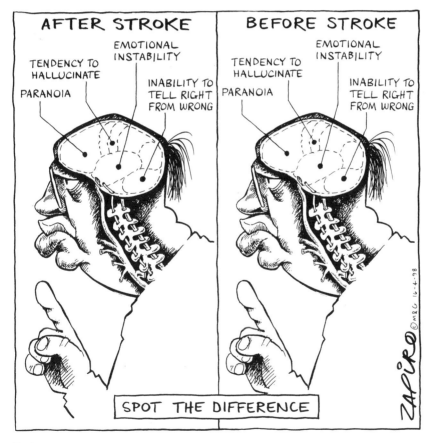

Zapiro

choose a final four – the winner, plus three runners-up. My fellow judges were a casting director (a woman) and someone involved in film (Richard).

Despite having watched many of these competitions before, I was rather unprepared for what followed. The master of ceremonies announced us. We were given seats in the cage immediately to one side of the stage, and Mr Scants 1990 was under way.

Each contestant walked out of the change room, did a quick sweep around the floor, spoke a couple of words to the MC, then vanished. I was still working on the second or third category – it's difficult to look, evaluate and score in about a minute – by the time the next contestant was on.

Despite this flurry, it was clear that the Mr Scants competitors did not all fit into the machoesque body-built mould. Actually, they ran the gamut of bulge and scrawn, tanned and lily-white, shy and exhibitionist. I wondered why there was a category called "appearance" on the judging sheet, since they were all naked but for scants. The "personality" category was useless: "What do you do?" the MC would ask semi-innocently, and the contestant would refuse to say.

After all the contestants had gone through their paces, they came out en masse and there was much craning from the judges' section as we tried to correspond the numbers on the bodies (artfully attached to the scants) to the numbers on the sheets and fill in all the blank spaces.

The casting director was asked to check to ensure there was no artifice in the bulges in the scants, much to the amusement of the crowd. One of the contestants had tried to cheat – he appeared on stage with a ribbon of toilet paper trailing from his scants.

Although there were 13 contestants, only a few had active support groups in the audience. One contestant was actually booed. "Ooh," said the MC, "you're a lot of bitches out there."

We were then given time to come up with our chosen finalists. I discovered to my horror that the casting director's mind was on other things and she had done very little in the way of scoring. Richard turned to me seriously and said: "Really, it has to be Number 4" – although by my sheet he barely scraped into the top seven.

After many comments by the MC along the lines of "the judges are having a tough time coming to a decision" – the judges were having a tough time totalling up the numbers in the five categories, thanks to the aforementioned bar service – we managed to come up with seven numbers. The casting director's contribution was limited to agreeing with everything Richard suggested.

When the faces (or rather underpants) corresponding to the numbers we'd chosen appeared, there were some obvious errors. Never mind – we had only to choose four finalists.

At this stage the "crowd response" category came to the fore. As each contestant strutted his stuff, the audience was encouraged to yell for its favourite. Some of the contestants' supporters had strategically situated themselves as close as possible to the cage, and trying to talk (or even think) became difficult as screams of "Number 7!" drowned out all else.

Richard persevered with his theory that Number 4 was the best and, for want of an alternative, I agreed. Number 4 it was, with Number 7 among the runners-up.

Amazingly, this haphazard method of judging seemed to satisfy everyone.

November 30 1990

Running the gladiator gauntlet
Angella Johnson

I had always considered exercise to be way overrated. Not for me the panting ache of pushing my body to the maximum, or the orgasmic high of an endorphin rush. At least that was before I bought into South Africans' fitness obsession and started working out like a lunatic.

So it was with a light heart that I greeted the news, from a fellow aerobics junkie, that auditions were being held for people to take part in the *Gladiators* television series to be aired on SABC3 next year.

For the uninitiated, *Gladiators* is a popular British game show (actually, it originated in the United States but matured after crossing the Atlantic) where sporting contestants pit themselves against serious "power athletes" in a series of energy-sapping exercises.

The South African version, I decided, would be an excellent opportunity to test my athletic prowess after several months of gruelling sessions with my Russian personal trainer.

But my enthusiasm evaporated when I walked into the department of physical education at Wits University for the try-outs – to find a classroom heaving with testosterone and a whiff of steroids.

Some 40-odd muscle-bulging bodies – chosen from more than 1 000 applicants – were anxiously awaiting a chance to shimmy up ropes, prance along balance beams, fling themselves off a 10m-high climbing frame, then run themselves ragged around a track. And that's just the half of it.

Keith Shaw, executive producer and rights holder in South Africa, warned us against overdoing it. (Not a problem for me.) "It's not the world wrestling championships," Shaw told us. "Enjoy the day and don't hurt yourselves. We know exactly what we're looking for."

What the show needed was good looks, height and a sparkling personality. These attributes were as important as physical prowess. Which frankly ruled out more than three-quarters of my fellow trialists.

"There are some very scary-looking people here," complained my female photographer with a shaky smile.

Yeah, especially a couple of young women whose neck size matched their waist measurements!

I was particularly fascinated by those who appeared to have shaved (and I'm talking chins here) that morning. Even their voices had a baritone quality.

Maybe someone up there wanted to punish me for my unkind thoughts, because, guess what, I ended up competing against a he-woman with a DDD bust (which clearly had not grown up with her) in an event called Power Ball.

She had to prevent me dumping some bright beach balls into baskets at either end of a hall, and then I had to stop her. It was a hopelessly unequal match. Wonder Boobs (they nestled rigidly and menacingly in a bright red spandex halter top) just brushed me off like a speck of dandruff.

That was only the beginning of my humiliation.

I failed to complete the 800m race because my bosom was having a painful race of its own. I also dropped out of the "seal run" – dragging my body across a field by walking on my hands like a seal.

But Gigi Schermoly, a wiry redhead from Fairland, Johannesburg, was no quitter. She rubbed her toes raw dragging her feet some 50m along the grass and could not put shoes on for four days afterwards.

In other events Schermoly, the world number eight in the pairs sports aerobics with partner Sergio Capellino (who just happens to be a tall, gorgeous gladiator called Spider), was short on strength. But she pranced on the balance beam as if it were the width of a boulevard.

I too had good balance. But as my score sheet later showed, I lacked the ability to do more than 13 parades on the beam during my two-minute time limit. I started to feel demoralisingly unfit next to these super-conditioned beings.

Take personal trainer Joanne Parnell, who came with an impressive curriculum vitae. A sturdy-looking lady, her titles include: reigning Miss Fitness SA, three times national Power Lifter champion, Miss Summertime 1997, Miss Coppertone SA and third place in Miss Bikini (Rand). Now she wants to be a gladiator. "It's something I've dreamed of all my life." (Funny, as it only started here last year – but maybe she thought this was another pageant.)

. Just when I had sized everyone up to be all brawn and minimal brain power, in stepped Anne Biccard, a former firefighter turned general practitioner and psychologist. "This is certainly not a career option, but I would love to be a gladiator or a contestant," she said. "Just for the fun of it. I just love competitive sports."

What did she think about the really dodgy-looking people with inflated biceps and leg muscles?

"I hope they get weeded out. The whole idea is that this should be a very clean family show. But they must have some kind of drug testing. You can't just discriminate because someone looks too muscular."

The TV series, described as a kind of one-on-one combat where male and female gladiators act as an obstacle to stop the competitors from achieving their goals, has been going for seven years in the United Kingdom. Hugely popular, it has turned regular participants with monikers like Wolf and Storm into household names; some even need bodyguards to stop people "testing" them out on the streets.

Arnold Dlamini, packed into a pale-blue lycra bodysuit, was hoping for similar stardom in South Africa. He was among a handful of black people taking part, a turnout that disappointed the organisers.

Dlamini, an unemployed clothing salesman, works out four times a week at the National Union of Mineworkers gym in Yeoville. "I'm a great sports fan, and I wanted to do this because it seems a very exciting life," he explained.

Three of the country's first gladiators – Jackal, Shaka (I guess he must be the black one) and Spider – were on hand to provide encouragement. Clad in figure-hugging lycra, which revealed their impressive buns, they were the standard to match.

"You've gotta be quick, fast, look good and work well with the camera," advised the Jackal, actor and computer software consultant Dave Riley. He also showed me the best way to climb a rope suspended from the gym's ceiling. "Use your legs for support and pull with your hands," he said. I tried, but could only manage to dangle from a knot at the end of the rope like the remaining piece of a broken baby mobile.

There were other failures throughout the day, but I shall spare my blushes.

Instead, let me share the only good thing written on my score sheet. My sit-ups (38 in two minutes compared with the 122 from Parnell) earned the comment: "Not very strong abdominal, but she fought hard to the end."

At last a sense of personal triumph. Not that I think it was worth the suffering. By the end of the five-hour trial I could hardly move my body. It felt as if I had Kryptonite poisoning. Every muscle in my body groaned with pain as I hobbled back to my office.

I woke up the following morning with a searing pain in my jaw and neck that lingered for days. Actually, my abs still ache – if only I had faked one of those sick notes from my mother that used to get me out of physical education classes at school.

October 2 1998

Making a date for cybersex
Mercedes Sayagues

Tuesday, April 6: An old flame who lives halfway around the world e-mails, professing eternal lust and shall we meet for cybersex at this website for shoe fetishists? Why not? says I. We make a date for Saturday at 10pm. I had been considering an upgrade of my e-mail link to full Internet. This is the perfect reason to do it.

Wednesday, April 7: Wrote cheque for Zim$999,90 to server, double the e-mail-only fee. Ready for some cyberaction.

Friday, April 9: Chose my cybername: lick my boots. Old flame's name: just do it.

Saturday, April 10, 9pm: Off to an early start and get sidetracked on a fetish search. The menu offers perplexing items. Latex sex: what is this, sex with a male condom on? No, people dressed in latex body suits, like vacuum-packed foie gras. Fistfucking: spare me that. Pregnant women having sex: I wonder if the stars keep getting pregnant to keep the job. Older women having sex: it is heartening to know one is not completely unemployable after age 70.

10pm: Log in. And what do I get? YOU NEED TO UPGRADE YOUR BROWSER. How in the world do I do this? E-mail a frantic SOS to server. Date flops.

Monday, April 12: Internet service provider manager Sydney sends instructions. Upgrading takes three boring hours. I follow instructions but still cannot access chat room. Instead I read the *Daily Mail & Guardian*, and check out latest info on Angola in six (not sex) sites. Since this year I have travelled to Angola more frequently than I got laid, I guess this makes sense. Downloading takes for ever. I am starting to hate the Internet.

Tuesday, April 13: Cyberlover tells me wild adventures with shoe fetishist he met in chat room and later in London. He attaches pics taken by co-fetishist. His instructions: "Winzip compacted, uncompact with Pkunzip, other format self-compacting (JPG)." What the hell does that mean? I hate cyberlover. Off to Bulawayo to do a story.

Friday, April 16: Back from Bulawayo. National holiday, long weekend. No reply from Sydney. He is surely having sex with his girlfriend. He does not need to upgrade his browser, he just pulls down his trousers. I hate Sydney.

Tuesday, April 20: Post and telecommunications (PTC) technicians on strike. Phone is dead. E-mail is dead. Internet is dead. I hate the PTC. Will change cybername to: neanderthal barefoot babe.

Monday, April 26: Strike is over. Workers win. Happy for them. *A luta continua* – Sydney replies! It will cost Zim$700 for a technician to upgrade my link. Will the *Mail & Guardian* pay so I can go on with story idea?

Tuesday, May 4: Tech Francis installs faster modem, but striking PTC workers sabotage server's dial-up lines: hooking takes up to an hour, lines drop constantly. Deep frustration.

Thursday, May 13: Server sorts out sabotage, but I still cannot access the web. Furious call to Francis's cellphone at 10pm, a gross lack of manners in

Zimbabwe. Crossed lines land my call on wife of wrong Francis, who turns out to be a bank executive. Wife does not believe I am looking for Francis the tech although I rattle angrily about connections before we realise the mistake.

Tuesday, May 18: Eureka! I'm having cybersex!

So how is it? I confess I had prejudices against cybersex. I thought I would end this piece with a disqualifier, like, better spend your money on a flimsy tanga. But, contrary to my expectations, there is something to be said for it.

There you are, writing your most secret thoughts, your dirtiest fantasies, the ones you would hesitate to whisper to your closest, hottest lover in bed.

Zapiro

There you go pouring it all to perfect strangers, protected by the anonymity of cyberspace (or so I hope).

After initial hesitations (what is the etiquette? what constitutes bad manners?), overcoming own shyness (do I really dare to write this?) and the ever-present guilt feeling (what if somebody walks in? what if my messages one day come to haunt me, like Bill Clinton's semen on a blue dress?), after a while I am into it, getting turned on by words and images. You reveal your sexual soul on the screen and someone, somewhere, plugs into your fantasies and responds in kind.

Or you plug into somebody else's. Like Bad Boy. He adores Princess Diana's and Fergie's feet (not Camilla's), posts pics of a shining, barefoot Di and makes up stories of weird sexual dalliances between Charles and Di.

So far, I have only seen softcore at this site. No torture scenes and no child porn. I wouldn't stomach these. I don't believe that stuff is protected under freedom of speech. It should be penalised, and I don't care if I sound like Tipper Gore.

Kinky sex it is. Monica, who wants to be told what underwear to wear to the office tomorrow. White Boots, who is turned on by women wearing these and collects their photos. Meshnet, who craves mock strangling with women's pantyhose. Nederlander likes to photograph feet in wrinkled pantyhose. Orango enjoys sniffing mules with pom-poms. The variety of foot and leg fetishes is mind-boggling.

The site is user-friendly. As I log in as New Kid on the Block, Naughty Boy explains how to "privately whisper to" for a liaison *à deux* (I hope). Unfortunately, sometimes I forget to hit it, so there go my words to all.

Most users enter, find a partner, and retreat into private whispering. Some post photos for all.

Zap among chat rooms – Boots Only, Socks and Pantyhose, Domination Lounge, Shoes and Sandals, Feet and Toes – with a caveat: you are playing musical chairs with 20 chatters per room. Either your slot is taken – or the line drops.

So what do you get out of it? A turn-on; a feeling of complicity with fellow chatters; a peek into other people's sexual fantasies, and into your own; a way to explore mental sex, unbound by physical presence and fleshy concerns.

Am I becoming a cyber-mystical Sor Juana Ines de la Cruz? OK, cut it out. It's just a way of passing the time when you have nothing more interesting to do.

The catch is that this is interesting. And safe: you won't catch Aids or get pregnant from cybersex. It's like visiting the S&M clubs of New York, without parking problems and for the cost of a local phone call.

It is fun to do it alone and fun to do it with a partner. I felt freer alone, when I could express my dirtiest thoughts, those you either keep secret or spill out to the world of cybersex addicts.

July 23 1999

We asked for captions for the following picture:

As usual, a good deal of the entries were unprintable. Most of the others dealt with the witches of Macbeth ("Bubble, bubble, toil and trouble ...").

Mark Potterton of Bedfordview sent in: "For a distinctive flavour add one ons-eie, two Nkamaties and a pinch of Rubicon. Don't stir too vigorously but do avoid browning. Serve with separate but equal amounts of raice".

Sue Owen of Rooiberg gave us: "This is a real South African stew ... of course there's no blerry black pepper in it".

M Zanni of Berea: "It's got all the Right ingredients. I assure you there won't be any Left".

S Jacobs of Gardens: "Government looks for credible (edible?) leaders to talk to. Can't find any. They're all in the stew".

Julian Stern of Observatory: "This Mossel Bay oil looks quite thick for my Mercedes" and "Oh, how I'd love to retire and become a chef at the Wimpy Bar".

M Crawford of Norwood sent in a range of answers, and came close to winning with this variation on the Macbeth theme: "Eye of Observer and toe of ITV, Newsweek's leg and Time's wing, For a charm of powerful trouble, Like a hell-broth boil and bubble".

She also gave us, "Pap and wors-e" and "S**t stirrer".

The prize went to Harald Strachan of Overport, Durban, for this offering: "Oh my God, it's Abramjee's femur".

A Ravan book is in the post.

Save your male
Ferial Haffajee

They were in need of a hard sell. Old favourites indeed, but a little frayed at the edges. So men needed rebranding, decided *Marie Claire* magazine recently.

The results of the advertisements for the men's competition appear in the magazine's November edition. They are a welcome break from the "exceptionally soothing cream for upset skin", "rehydrating" this and "rejuvenating" that advertising which pollute the pages of glossies.

Men, like floy discs and vinyl records, are almost obsolete. What with their lower sperm counts, the recent Constitutional Court breakthroughs on artificial insemination and the glass ceiling shattering around women on the fast track, men need all the communications help they can get.

Gitam International went phallic: they remind women that cacti are all pricks, that bananas go off and that vibrators run down.

Network's offering is more cerebral: their ad features three half-titled books called *Juliet, Cleopatra* and *Bonnie,* the unstated pay-off line obviously being what would women be without Romeo, Antony and Clyde.

The office favourite is Herdbuoys's "Save-the-Male" campaign which offers women a cut-out mask of Brad Pitt to use on your husband or partner when he may have "gone bald. His bag of bedroom tricks run empty."

October 31 1997

Son of a beach
Shaun de Waal

Inevitably, once Leonardo DiCaprio got involved, the making of *The Beach* became a major gossip-fest. Allegations flew about the film-makers' ecological destruction of the beach where it was being filmed in Thailand; and Leo had allegedly hired an entire island nearby to house his current girlfriend.

The rumours that impinge more plausibly on the film itself have to do with – let's be blunt – Leo and his torso. Director Danny Boyle and scriptwriter John Hodge originally thought of Ewan McGregor, who made his name in their superb *Shallow Grave* and brilliant *Trainspotting*, to play the lead in *The Beach*. But when DiCaprio indicated an interest in the film, the Hollywood money-men made Boyle an offer he couldn't refuse – to substantially enlarge the film's budget.

So DiCaprio was signed. And, so the gossip goes, Leo was obliged – since he'd be spending much of the movie half-dressed – to get his body toned up. It wouldn't do to let his adoring *Titanic* public see the flabby results of his playboy lifestyle. Oh, the responsibilities of a sex symbol!

True or not, these stories colour one's perception of *The Beach*, possibly with good reason. It's almost as though Boyle decided to reassure the audience early on that DiCaprio had managed to slim down and buff up sufficiently, as we get a stripped-to-the-waist shot of him within the movie's first few minutes. Whew. Okay, we'll watch it.

After that, viewing this tale of how a group of backpackers find an idyllically isolated tropical paradise, and how it all goes wrong, one has a strange sense of slippage as to what *The Beach* is actually about. Is it about how uncontained desire and the need for social policing will always compromise any human attempt at recreating Eden? Or is it about Leo's (admittedly pretty) torso?

As it happens, the film is a fine adaptation of Alex Garland's bestselling novel, though it simplifies the plot and adds more sex – in the book, there's a pervasive feeling of unfulfilled longing. We also have less of a sense than in the novel of how his character's flirtation with the romance of the Vietnam War creeps into psychosis.

It works, in general, though how it all turns out will surprise neither the many who read the novel nor those who know William Golding's classic *Lord of the Flies*, which is so often mentioned in connection with *The Beach*.

This is expert storytelling and slickly inventive film-making, yet one comes away from the movie with a feeling of something missing.

Perhaps it's the lack of an actor with real depth to carry the lead role; one can't help wondering how much better *The Beach* might have been with McGregor as the protagonist. DiCaprio is okay, despite the fact that he can't entirely overcome the liability of his inherently smug little face. But he should be more than just okay. Maybe the time he could have spent exploring the nuances of his character were instead spent refining the nuances of his torso.

February 18 2000

A walk on the wild side
Mercedes Sayagues

Kuda was upset. He felt the police were harassing him. So he walked into Harare Central police station, dressed in a pink miniskirt and a long, curly wig.

"Is there a problem with the way I dress?" he asked. The police let him go. They must have been awestruck at the sight of a Shona man, 1,9m in height and weighing more than 100kg, dressed in drag.

Certainly I was awestruck when I first met Kuda. In his drag personality ("Yvonne Chaka Chaka"), the outgoing Jacaranda Queen of Zimbabwe makes a stunning impression. Her huge styrofoam breasts busting out of her strapless top, she leans over to kiss me on the cheek. She is regal in a burgundy Victorian crinoline skirt, massive platform boots, and the crown and ribbon befitting her title.

A few weeks ago, Kuda tearfully passed over her crown to Peter, aka Naomi, at the Jacaranda Queen contest, Zimbabwe's premier drag event. I was invited to be one of three judges.

I ask Kuda if his size is ever a problem with men. "Not at all," he says. "African men like big women. I embody their fantasy."

Kuda (27) was once married ("I trained myself to fuck my wife while having my own fantasies"), had a daughter ("African tradition requires an heir and I am a traditional girl") and came out of the closet in this flamboyant reincarnation ("I am the Queen of Africa!").

Holly came from Miami, Fla,
hitchhiked her way across the USA
plucked her eyebrows on the way,
shaved her legs and then he was a she,
and she said, hey, babe, take a walk on the wild side.

How do you define a queen? I ask.

"Anyone in stilettos wearing a fabulous outfit," shrieks Queen Naomi (23).

"An effeminate gay man who takes a woman's role in bed and in life," says Romeo (27), voted Miss Personality. "I want to be treated and cared for like a woman."

Would they want a sex change or do they wish to have been born a woman? A unanimous No!

"Women are so oppressed here," sighs first princess Chester. "I have more fun as I am."

Are you a man or a woman? "The magic is having both sexes," says Naomi. "Men like to play with the mouse and boot the computer." I must look blank because he hastens to explain: "Men like to play with my dick and then open the box." He gestures to his behind.

"What is a man, what is a woman?" muses Chester. "I challenge sexual identity. I am what I choose to be." Adds fashion designer Peter, who was voted Miss Safe Sex as Marie-Jose: "If men identified more with women, there would be less violence and oppression in society."

Candy came from out on the Island
In the backroom she was everybody's darling
But she never lost her head
Even when she was giving head.
She said, hey honey, take a walk on the wild side.

Straight-looking gay men can blend. Queens don't fit. They are a sub-genre within a subculture. Perhaps this is why they live on a hysterical edge, with wild mood swings.

"Queen politics is to debunk the world, to turn everything on its head, so they are constantly reacting against society," says Keith Goddard, chair of Gays and Lesbians of Zimbabwe (Galz).

"It's like living with Maria Callas. When they are not making a scene, they are applying make-up," says one boyfriend. "You can't imagine the shit I have to put up with, the arguments, the jealous fits. But I enjoy it."

Most have steady partners, white and black, straight and gay, older and younger. They also have affairs and endless dramas. "It's painful to be a queen, we are heartbroken all the time," says Romeo. He explains that queens fall passionately in love with men who ultimately leave them to get married and have children.

"We waste our time on high life and glamour instead of building strong relationships. Who will take care of us in our old age? Old queens end up paying for a boyfriend, it's so sad," he says.

Jackie has just been away
Thought she was James Dean for a day
Then I guess she had to crash
Valium would have helped that pass.
Hey sugar, take a walk on the wild side.

Backstage at the Jacaranda Queen contest, Shona and Ndebele reign. All 15 contestants are black or brown. If there were any doubts, this seals the indigenisation of the gay question in Zimbabwe.

The contest is an elaborate affair at a posh venue in Harare, complete with catwalk, lights, MC, guests and a wild party afterwards.

For the beauty contest, the queens sashay in swimwear, daywear and evening gowns. These are dazzling, couturier-style affairs.

Queen Naomi wore a skimpy brassiere and miniskirt in shocking-pink fake fur and a transparent organza jacket. The first princess wore a slinky, sequinned black gown and an extravagant tulle hat with a long veil. Miss Personality dazzled in a light-pink satin number with a short skirt in front and a long hem behind – very John Galliano.

Marie-Jose wore a romantic, *Gone with the Wind*-style cream gown with a long train, petticoats, and white buds marking the low decolleté.

On the talent part, the jury asked participants if they would prefer to be Winnie Madikizela-Mandela, Grace Mugabe or Monica Lewinsky, and why. Winnie trailed Monica, who was admired for reaping fame and money from giving the United States president a blow job.

Queen Naomi says she will raise funds for Galz during her reign, and liberate all drag queens so people will take them seriously.

Given the homophobic climate in Zimbabwe, the queens tell of a surprising degree of tolerance and acceptance from their families and neighbours.

Chester came out in Nyazura, a small town in the eastern highlands, and found himself accepted, even at church. But he had to fight it alone. It is easier in Highfield, a working-class township of Harare, where he shares a house with his boyfriend, a soldier. Neighbours presume they are a couple. The soldier, however, removes his uniform before coming home.

"Who says this is not African? Culture changes," says Chester, aka Lady De'Jonge.

Most queens are militant gay activists. It takes courage, under Zimbabwe's repressive government, to walk in drag into Harare Central. Or into Harare's downtown discos.

Queens and a handful of committed gay women form the core of Galz. "You can always count on the queens to stage a demo," says Galz staff member Romeo.

Pity Canaan Banana. If only he had been president these days, how much consensual fun he could have had. Just by taking a walk on the wild side.

December 18 1998

It's a doll's world
Khadija Magardie

To be honest, I've always wondered how she manages to do it.

Barbie, that is.

With her impressive, nipple-free bosom more than twice the size of her waist, equally impressive legs more than twice as long as her torso, and feet so femininely tiny that she can neither balance nor stand on them, she is every man's fantasy. But all of these attributes have, no doubt, been a great disadvantage for the peroxided blonde in her many careers.

After all, since her launch over 40 years ago, Barbie has been very busy out there in the world – she has done stints as a beauty queen, a dancer, a surgeon and an air stewardess – to name a few.

By now, Barbie the career girl will have found out that one can seldom be effective in the workplace with men staring down your chest all day, or by tottering around the construction site in stilettos.

Now doll-makers have cottoned on to the idea of "the PC doll". This trend subscribes to the idea that in order to make a doll more popular, especially among "non-Aryans", she must look more realistic. Particularly, she is supposed to look more "like a real woman".

Of course, Barbie, the descendant of a swimsuit-clad German porno doll called Lili, is not about to change overnight. She may come in black, Hispanic or Oriental models, but her bodily proportions and her lifestyle remain the same. She is, of course, career-minded and gym-oriented, and despite their long relationship, nuptials with lifelong beau Ken are not on the horizon.

Last month, at a local trade show, a newcomer, "Palesa", walked away with the "toy of the year" award. The doll, described by her creators as "a true African princess", has a bigger butt, fuller breasts and hips, and is said to represent "a new generation of African women.

Palesa comes with her own range of ethnic wear. As listed in her impressive CV, Palesa is "feminine, a successful academic, and an independent woman".

It would be interesting to think of the future of dolldom if the little nymphettes would really start looking like the rest of us.

Picture it. Home Executive Heidi, resplendent in hair curlers, nicotine-stained lips, and balancing an infant or two on each wide hip. Of course, this doll would have her own wardrobe of interchangeable overalls, each splattered with leftover baby food, or cooking oil. Listed as accessories would be a vacuum cleaner, an ashtray and perhaps a telephone.

Or Check-out Cindy, with over-bleached hair, and gaudy blue eyeshadow. Of course, Cindy would have a special hole in her lips to blow bubblegum. And she would have flat feet, suitable for wearing sensible walking shoes. Maybe she could even have varicose veins.

Take your pick ...

What about Domestic Debbie? Debz should have a blue-checkered housecoat, with a matching doek, and a blanket around her torso, safety-pinned at the chest. Accessories? A gurgling blonde infant to put inside the blanket; plus a matchbox-size room "out back", with a cast-iron bed, and no windows. For an optional extra, the manufacturers could throw in a madam that shrills "Debyyyyyyyyyyyy, where are my earrings?" in a nasal (maybe Sandton) accent.

Strictly for South African toy-shelves, we will have Talk-Show Tiffany, who will have a wardrobe full of Chanel-style power suits, and a choice of red nail polishes. If you press a button at the back, the doll will start repeating "When I was in the States ..." and flutter her eyelashes incessantly. Beneath the suits, which will be skilfully sewn to disguise every bulge and wobble, the doll will have additional soft bits on her thighs, breasts and butt, which are removable. The little girl who buys the doll can remove these parts if she wants, but she would have to buy a whole new wardrobe for her doll, which manufacturers will have specially designed. The doll will come with a rudimentary video camera that can be operated by anyone, but that will only record when it is focused on the doll.

We could also have Government-Office Geena, who will have a vast array of pastel print frocks and hand-knitted jerseys, but only one pair of shoes – white patent leather pumps, with scuffed heels. Geena will have a special pair of battery-operated hair tongs that can electrify her hair, and a little compact that contains only ruby-coloured face powder. Geena's accessories could be a Walkman, so that she can pretend to not understand any word that is said to her, and a magazine rack containing back issues of *Huisgenoot* that she can busy herself with during office hours.

Most necessarily, the bodies of these "real" dolls would be something for little girls to think about.

Perhaps Heidi's breasts could be made a little like the empty bags that are tell-tale signs of years of lactation. Maybe she could have some white stretch-marks carved into her lower abdomen.

It would be nice if some of the dolls could have cellulite, too, just a little around the buttocks. Of course, one will be able to buy a vanity bag as an accessory, filled with toners, astringents, packs and massage gloves. Maybe the makers could even include a treadmill.

Because of morality, one supposes it would be asking too much that the doll sprout a few pubic hairs, or maybe have some bristles on her lower lip or chin. One could, I suppose, include a razor or depilatory.

If her feet were flat, and not designed for the high heels that do little for the posture, and are unsuitable for walking long distances, the doll would be a lot more comfortable. After all, she could then fetch the kids from school with ease, or stand for hours hawking vegetables in Sauer Street. But then, of course, one would need to include some corns or bunions on the feet.

The bottom line when it comes to dolls is that the further from the natural female form, the more feminine and hence acceptable she is.

Dolls cannot and, for marketing purposes, will never mirror reality. The deflated breasts and orange-peel thighs of the majority of the world's women will look obscene on a figurine that caters exclusively for fantasy. It is laughable that dolls now claim to look like the women of the world, when in fact, the manufacturers are merely changing the icing on the same cake.

Last year, some feminists got excited when a partnership between two US dairy produce giants came up with Milkmaid Barbie. The doll was kitted out in a Holstein-cow print overall shorts, and was clutching a milk carton. But beneath the wrappings, it was the same good old Barbie. Manufacturers assured the public that this was no lactating doll – there was, alas, no breast-pump included either ...

March 21 2000

Part Four
The Body Politic

Trailblazing along the cul-de-sac to glory
Steven Friedman

And now a watershed manifesto from the State Precedent (so called because we have no option but to follow him).

"Friends, Natalians, countrymen, lend me your fears. I come to bury expectations, not to raise them.

"Several days ago, I sent my foreign minister to Vienna and the local media with a reform package which I promised to outline this evening.

"Unfortunately, the package had no strings attached and this made it a difficult burden to carry; in the best traditions of the post office, it came apart before we could deliver it. I also discovered that the changes we had promised would plunge our beloved country into chaos, poverty and despair at the behest of meddling foreigners. There is no need to do this when we have already achieved these goals by our own efforts.

"I have therefore decided to depart from tonight's scheduled programme in which I was expected to blaze a new trail and to leave you instead with the trailer. Those who demand the main features can go to blazes.

"The poet Langenhoven (Frik Langen-hoven, the Publications Appeal Bard), wrote that 'no news is good news'. Surely this sage advice applies to reform too? It demands that I rise to the challenge and reveal to you tonight the many sweeping changes I intend not making in the days ahead.

"In response to the needs of the time, I have decided, with immediate effect, not to release Mandela, negotiate with real black leaders or abolish influx control. These are not easy decisions not to have made, but I can assure you that we will follow this path of riotousness with a new sense of emergency.

"Until tonight, the task which faces us has been difficult, but not impossible. I believe the steps I have not outlined will rectify this error and ensure that we turn this wilderness of ours into a just desert.

"This is indeed a watershed; if you have water, prepare to shed it now."

August 23 1985

Average white supremacists?
Krisjan Lemmer

I saw this logo the other day which, I must say, stopped me in my tracks:

Then I thought – oh, clearly AWB post-Jani Allan but pre-Paardekraal. Then I looked closer – just the work of some long-haired rockers called the Average White Band.

No relation, I hope.

April 27 1990

Watch that raindrop – it could be the pope

Gus Silber

Thousands of pilgrims of all faiths and colours did not flock to Lesotho to see the pope last week because they knew the entire beatification ceremony would be broadcast live on M-Net.

Immediately after this historic event thousands of pilgrims of all faiths and colours flocked to Lesotho in order to escape the possibility of a repeat broadcast.

Zapiro

This was not the pope's fault. Indeed, one felt relieved that His Holiness had been in a position where he was unable to watch himself live on M-Net, for he might otherwise have been forced to revoke his blanket blessing on all the people of Southern Africa.

For this exclusive live broadcast was not exactly a blessed event.

Cursed by rain, gremlins, timid camerawork, mismatched commentary and confused direction, it was an unholy mess that marked former *Netwerk* anchorman Kollie van Koller's baptism by damp squib into the fiery world of independent television production.

Having secured exclusive rights for coverage of the pope's Lesotho visit, he somehow neglected to secure cameramen who knew where to find the pope and soundmen who knew how to fix a short-circuit.

The result was a fuzzy, buzzy, blurring demonstration of the fallibility of man in the presence of a force beyond his control: TV.

In the beginning, there was a slide show starring the pope. "His Holiness the Pope is here in Southern Africa," twinkled an awed female voice, "what a privilege!"

The pope beamed and blessed people of diverse ethnic origins. Her Ickiness the Commentator wondered why. "This charismatic universal father of all Christian churches, this unique, intensely caring man, why is he so loved, and what is it about him that is so forcefully dynamic?"

Perhaps it was his forceful dynamism. Soon we would have a chance to find out for sure. The camera cut to a racecourse in the shadow of a mountain in Maseru, where millions of worshippers awaited the arrival of the pontiff. Well, hundreds of thousands. Well, tens of thousands. Well, 10 000.

"A great crowd has gathered in the paddock," confirmed commentator Mark Lloyd, as the camera carefully confined its roaming to the area where the crowd was most thickly concentrated.

Then the camera lost its concentration in the panic of the first official sighting of the popemobile. Then it lost focus. Then it lost popemobile.

Then picture lost sound. A conductor flapped his arms with gusto, a choir opened their mouths, and nothing came out.

"We are working to improve the sound quality of our live transmission," confessed a running message at regular intervals.

Sound was found, but it wasn't much of an improvement. "The pope will be approaching the high altar from the north and the west," navigated Mark Lloyd. The pope approached. "The motorcade is now travelling south along the eastern perimeter of this vast racecourse." Despite these explicit directions the cameraman remained unable to locate the exact whereabouts of His Holiness.

Then a miracle occurred. The pope found the cameras. But even he wasn't able to do anything about their focus. Off-camera, he changed from his white cloak into his white cloak.

"The Holy Father has changed from his zucchetto into his mitre, from his soutane into his gothic chasible," pontificated Mark Lloyd, clearly grateful something of note was happening at last.

But the costume change made it even more difficult for the cameramen to recognise the Bishop of Rome. In order to keep their options open, they ensured that the pope, if indeed it was the pope, was at all times partially obscured by someone else's head or elbow, or at least hidden in overcast half-light under the papal canopy.

The rest of the time, they forgot about the pope altogether, fixing their focus on the papal canopy for as long as it took to fall asleep.

Then it rained and people put up their own canopies all over the place. Blobs of drizzle slid across the surface of the lens, although the difference between these blobs and those under the papal canopy was merely academic. People presented the pope with gifts. We saw rear views of the people, and no views of the gifts. Or the pope. If indeed it was the pope.

September 23 1988

This country is closed on account of bad weather
Steven Friedman

And now, as the rand sinks quickly in the West, we bring you the Worm cure-all fiscal plan guaranteed to restore our currency to its rightful place alongside the Polynesian conch shell.

We all know that the board of Botha Disinvestments was recently forced to close the economy until further notice after our chief executive's orational outburst in Durban prompted a sharp drop in international Rubiconfidence. Foreign banks now want their money back and the recent transformation of our banknotes into suicide notes means we are unable to pay them.

In other words, we face the political bankruptcy long predicted by our national profit, Piet Koornhof, who revealed several years ago that "apartheid is debt".

The usual solution would be to liquidate the nation (Minister Le Grange has already volunteered for the job) and allow our creditors to take over our assets. The problem is that we no longer have any. But one thing we do have in abundance is liabilities, and we can solve both our economic and political problems by selling them off instead.

Yes, fellow shareholders, the only course open to us is to allow the foreign banks to repossess PeeWee himself. This will not only provide our only hope of an internationally accepted settlement but will allow us to wash our rands of the burden they have been carrying.

Once the banks own the national Albatross, they will be free to use him in any way they choose – this will be their Own Affair. They may even prefer to lend him to some suitable government such as the Paraguayan, thus making the deal a Loan Affair, but this is unlikely as the rate of interest in PeeWee has dropped sharply ever since he put his manifesto in his mouth.

There is a real danger, then, that our offer might not satisfy them. If so, this Worm suggests that we throw in a few generals as well, provided we can obtain the necessary general dealer's licence. They can also have the

Broederbond but, at the current bond rate, they might prefer not to.

While we're about it, we might as well get the randwagon rolling again by flogging off the entire Cabinet and National Party caucus, a Nat loss which our national accounts should be able easily to absorb. In other words, the only solution to our economic woes is a final Natal sell-out and we in the trade even have a name for this imaginative solution.

It's called flogging a dead horse.

September 6 1985

An intravenous critique of gradualistic punctuation
Thomas Equinus

Mystics refer to ecstatic experiences as "moments out of time". I haven't been able to relate to temporally unbound ecstasy since I caught the blonde looking at her watch behind my head. My friend by proxy, Klaas de Jonge, disagrees: "Sure there are moments outside time. I forget all about time and place when I'm playing darts and table tennis or feeding my tropical fish. What else is there to do in Pretoria, anyway?"

Classical theology tells us that only God is without beginning or end and lives in a kind of timeless present. The rest of us are left to clutch at Epiphanies which are all too time-bound and irremedially momentary. However, we do have one advantage over God in that we get to have weekends. For God reality is eternally fixed at 10am on Thursday and someone's left Radio 5 on.

Time is my theme this week, oh persons in Christ. And let me immediately congratulate D Mackenzie, of Melville, for winning the Spot-the-Deliberate-Mistake competition. Of course Kierkegaard could not have opened the Oslo Trade Fair in 1673 (line 2). He was not alive in 1673. His dates are 1813-1855.

D Mackenzie also perspicaciously pointed out that my new column included two trendy non-sequiturs, a dangling paragraph and an unrelated pronoun. However, I reject his contention that my sixth paragraph represented an attempt to subversively promote Fabian Gradualism via subordinate clauses. The Gradualism was in the punctuation marks, especially the gratuitous commas. This mistake apart, Mackenzie is to be commended, and a copy of *Boy's Onanist Annual* will be mailed to him shortly.

The clue to the deliberate mistake was in the description "period philosophy" in line 33. For, as Noam Chomsky said in 1843: "The whole point of doing period philosophy is to get the period right; by 'period' I do not mean the full stop, a punctuation mark much hated by the Fabian Society. You can always spot a creeping socialist by his propensity for using the semicolon and the conjunction 'and', just as Marxists always write 'god' with an uncapped 'g' and medical men use spastic colons. My wife, on the other hand, is inclined to use the exclamation mark and the interrogative sentence, especially when I come home late, and she can only be pacified by my dangling participle."

Chomsky chose the International Forum of Lesbians Against Peace as the occasion for the exposure of this piece of wisdom. Like all academics he was out of touch with reality and couldn't understand why he was carried from the hall and hung upside down in a broom cupboard for two weeks. A moderate faction's slim two-vote majority swung the ballot on intravenous feeding and when Chomsky was discovered by a yogic hippy looking for a vertical bed for the night, he was still coherent and managed three run-on lines, 12 expletives and a diphthong before lapsing into the individual unconscious.

The yogi, soft in the head after a furious summer in Athens, set Chomsky's broom-cupboard speech to music and the song became a surprise hit in Luxembourg when played backwards. However, the sheet music was declared to be subversive and the vice squad ordered that nipple-caps be placed on the full stops. Fabian Gradualism was further eliminated by changing the time signature. As originally written, the chorus was to be repeated 74 times, ending only after a sustained mantra including the words "Hey Jude" in Gujarati. The song was particularly popular with DJs, who would put it on and then go to the movies.

Having somewhat more time than those DJs on my hands, I went to Jameson's public house in the early hours of Saturday morning to pursue my speculations on time. I should have been asleep, but I wanted to see which intrepid fellow denizens of the concrete jungle scorned the conventional dictates of clock-time. Bleary-eyed, I spotted a familiar face – Bruce Fordyce's. "Bruce," I said, "you're a man who knows about time. You're famous because once a year, between 6am and 12 noon, you cover a particular distance in a brilliant time. Is there a timeless moment or is reality fastened to the specifications of linear progression?"

Fordyce looked at me blankly, hiccuped, and said, "Your question is very interesting, whoever you are. But I'm sick and tired of talking about the Comrades Marathon. I've won it so many times that my curiosity is satisfied.

Derek Bauer

What I need to know now is whether I can drink 10 whiskies and stand on one leg." He then attempted to stand on one leg and failed. "Don't worry," he belched, "I've still got five whiskies to go."

On Sunday morning I started off at four minutes a kilometre in the Commercial Union 21 and was feeling great until Bruce Fordyce came jogging past with no apparent effort, quipping about the unseasonal winter heat hampering his pace. I realised that I'd have at least 15 minutes more PT out there than he would. And I further realised that between the desire and the spasm, the foreplay and the afterglow, the first whiskey and the tenth, the pity and the terror, the starting gun and the winning post Falls the Shadow: Life can be very long, as can sentences by the Fabian Gradualists and the ramblings of regular *WM* columnists.

July 31 1987

Tour of the killing fields
Krisjan Lemmer

You know, nobody has greater respect for the truth than Oom Krisjan does. So when protesters in the United States claim that the South African Tourist Board's promotion in their country isn't quite accurate – expansive game parks, happy natives - I can't in all honesty quarrel.

But what's the alternative? The American Committee on Africa took particular exception to the promise of "exotic Kalahari Bushmen". Why, they ask, is there "no mention of the systematic and genocidal extermination of San and Khoisan-speaking peoples and cultures by successive white supremacist regimes"?

OK – but I'm struggling to visualise the revised advert.

September 21 1990

The Republic of ParaNoya

Steven Friedman

To: Editor

From: Suspended Worm temporarily in disused mineshaft in independent homeland of KwaDeserted to avoid subversion. Have ducked all responsibilities by taking chicken run and can be reached at Hotel Extravaganza, Assumption, ParaNoya, a small South American republic on the border of Sanity. First dispatch follows. Patriotic regards.

Assumption, ParaNoya. An unbelievable calm has settled on this fantasy-rich enclave after its ruling elite's recent shock decision to declare peace on its citizenry.

Pickled observers in the bar lounge of the Hotel Extravaganza agree that the violence which has plagued this relative democracy – its government is elected by the president and several of his relatives – has now been entirely banished from its newspapers and television screens, and in the words of one official, "placed firmly back on the streets where it belongs".

Part of the government's unique achievement lies in its decision to allow security forces to arrest all inhabitants of the capital, Assumption, without a warrant: "The government's claims to have restored peace," noted one observer, "are based entirely on an unwarranted Assumption."

But the authorities themselves ascribe much of their success to the appointment of Signora Florencia "Flo" d'Informacion as Newsmaker of the Year, charged with the sole responsibility for making the news. In only a few days, Signora d'Informacion has restored national consensus by consensoring all news items which differ from the official subversion of events disseminated by the government's Department for the Reconstruction of Reality.

Miss d'Informacion's formal title is National Steward of the Truth. While she makes the news two other stewards assist her by complaining about all reports emanating from non-governmental sources – they are known colloquially as "whine stewards".

As one Cabinet minister put it: "Experience has shown that there is no better way of getting people to see things your way than appointing a steward."

In an attempt to rebut charges that it has imposed censorship, the government insists that the steward appear in public surrounded at all times by a detachment of troops – evidence, it insists, that "our security forces are here to protect the free Flo d'Informacion".

In an exclusive interview this week – all questions were excluded by military decree – the Free Flo discussed the work of her deception committee. In an attempt to dispel the forbidding image of her painted by ParaNoya's critics, she responded to all hostile questions with a quick gag.

"Our chief aim," she explained, looking nervously over her shoulder at her chief, "is to dispel our image as a banana republic. From now on we will be a corn republic instead and will feed our subjects on corn alone. To this end, we have already devised an elaborate maize to still dissent. The trick is to build public confidence and a department like my own is uniquely suited to achieving this confidence trick."

Miss D'Informacion noted that her committee had also boosted public morale by its recent edict prescribing strict penalties for members of the public who become depressed about the curbs she has introduced. "By cracking down on depress freedom, we have ensured a cheerier nation," she noted. "One swallow may not make a summer, but it's amaizing what people will swallow when threatened with a summons." The decree has worked, she said, because in ParaNoya, "the edictor's decision is final".

ParaNoya's people would now be able to rid themselves of fear in the knowledge that "there is no better security blanket than a good dose of blanket security".

The steward also noted that the new dispensation had been introduced to quell mounting foreign criticism of ParaNoya, a goal which had already been achieved. "It's only a matter of time before the world officially sanctions us," she predicted.

Miss d'Informacion acknowledged that ParaNoya's "New Information Order"

– in which all information can only appear by official order – may appear stringent to outsiders. But it was necessary, she insisted, "to counter the scourge of Marx".

This is believed to be a reference to a beetle-browed comedian and long-serving ParaNoya Cabinet minister, whose trademark is a shambling walk. It was he who devised the current ParaNoya government policy, designed to counter the worldwide columnist menace with a strategy known in security circles as "total shambles".

In conclusion, the Free Flo stressed her government's continuing commitment to individual rights. "We are determined to stamp out the heard mentality by ensuring that nothing at all is heard. The liberty of all our subjects will be assured as long as we in the government guard the right to No," she added.

Miss d'Informacion has no previous convictions. Since she assumed office, she has ensured that the people of ParaNoya no longer have any either.

The public of ParaNoya were unavailable for comment at the time this report went to supPress.

NOTE: Like all reports from ParaNoya, this one is entirely fictitious. Any coincidence between the world described by the Free Flo and that outside her office is entirely coincidental.

July 4 1986

The Johnny and Ronnie Show

Charlotte Bauer

If they ever decided to take up a comedy career, John Bishop and Ronnie Kasrils would make a good pair.

Like Laurel and Hardy, Cheech and Chong and the Blues Brothers before them, Ronnie and Johnny could play up their differences until the house comes down.

Their props would be minimal – a styrofoam truncheon and British "Bobby" helmet for Johnny and a wooden AK-47 and "Beatle" cap for Ronnie.

Lenin himself was fond of the "Beatle" cap long before The Beatles were born. He wore one to hide his receding hairline. Ronnie could wear it at a jauntier angle to hide his wriggling eyebrows which look rather like two copulating mescal worms in a puddle of tequila.

As a comedy duo, they wouldn't have to do much more than buff up the script they rehearsed on Sunday night's *Agenda*.

Johnny: "I used to be a policeman, you know."

Ronnie: "You should have warned me – maybe I should break out of the studio."

In a burlesque routine, such dialogue might be amusingly accompanied by Johnny chasing Ronnie into the stalls with his truncheon while Ronnie flees up the aisle singing the *Internationale* while beating time on his own head with a string of pork sausages.

One of the questions Bishop asked Kasrils on *Agenda* could also be built neatly into a double-act.

Johnny: "I say, I say, I say, what's the difference between the communist party and the ANC?"

Ronnie: "I've no idea. But have you seen how I can rub my tummy and pat my head at the same time?"

(Drum roll, cymbal clash.)

Ronnie: "Here's one for you Johnny: Knock knock."

Johnny: "Who's there?"

Ronnie: "Freak."

Johnny: "Freak who?"

Ronnie: "Freak Robinson!"

(Canned laughter, comb-and-paper sound effects.)

While all this was going on in the *Agenda* studio, rigged up to transmit live from the African National Congress conference in Durban, the rest of the debating team were making strenuous efforts to strike a more serious note.

Jacob Zuma, Cyril Ramaphosa and Pallo Jordan declined to climb on the bandwagon, rise to the bait or otherwise get funny with Bishop, not even when he asked Zuma to tell everyone a bit about himself "as a human being".

Zuma resisted the temptation to say that he was really an extraterrestrial agent sent down by the Jupiter Freedom Party for the Liberation of the Third Moon.

Similarly, Ramaphosa refused to be reeled in by Bishop's trout fishing metaphor or by the SABC TV "Twenty Questions" game which invariably starts with "Are you a communist?"

Instead, both he and Pallo Jordan, in particular, really did their damndest to explain things in a way that might pre-empt the same stupid old questions in future. Seldom, at least on television, have I heard the ANC's case put so eloquently. Between the two of them, they managed to rise way above the occasion, never mind the bait.

My only criticism of Ramaphosa is that, as the debate hotted up, he started wagging his right index finger, a disturbing mannerism which brought back bad memories of an awful little man who used to wave his digit about so wildly it did permanent damage to both the country and the second joint.

All in all, it was a ripping good show, brought to a close with a final turn from Ronnie and Johnny. Calling time-out for another week, Johnny made ready to go, looking as jolly and pleased with himself as he usually does at this point.

"I always have the last word," he said.

"I'll have the last laugh, then," responded Ronnie, quick as a flash. (More laughter, cymbal roll, general percussion noises, applause.)

I trust there was a talent scout in the audience.

July 2 1991

Dear Walter

David Beresford

SAS OUTENIQUA – SHIP'S LOG

FRIDAY May 9, 08h00. Set sail from Simonstown under command Captain Horatio Mbeki, Rear Admiral Nelson (that's me) on board.

18h00. Frustrating day. Still as a painted ship upon a painted ocean. Altercation between Captain Mbeki and First Mate Modise over whether the purchase of boat from cousin in Kiev was inclusive of engine. Oars supplied do not reach water. Albatross perched on the forecastle keeps winking at me. Bears uncanny resemblance to my guru, Paidrag O'Sullivan. Wonder if it is a message from beyond?

Saturday 10h00. Captain does hornpipe in attempt to revive flagging morale. Captain overboard. Lifeboat lowered. Sinks without trace. Captain clambers up anchor chain. Failure to raise anchor identified as major factor behind lack of progress. Set sail to cheers from inebriated press corps on quay. Captain orders First Mate keelhauled.

17h00. Break open grog ration. Captain overboard.

20h00. Assuming command I open sealed orders: "Proceed to heart of " I immediately issue orders to head for Port Noire-by-the-Sea.

B.P.

Sunday 09h00. Crow's nest spots unidentified bobbing object. Divert and discover raft carrying our bedraggled Captain in extremis. Says disappearance overboard ploy to facilitate shuttle diplomacy. Forgot shuttle. Survived by eating albatross. Bodes ill for our voyage. As Paidrag always used to say: "There's no such thing as a free lunch, except for the editor of *The Star*."

12h00. Captain in delirium, screaming: "Save Sacs!" Roll-call confirms nobody called Sacs on board. Captain clapped in irons for own safety. Ship's doctor prescribes hourly administration of industrial solvent. Hair falls out after first dose. Don't know about Aids, but will never sell as shampoo.

15h00. Land ahoy! Through eyeglass I see two bands of savages fighting on beach. Ordered poop gun to fire single round over their heads. Cannon ball lands amidships, splintering second lifeboat. General hilarity on beach, resulting in suspension of hostilities. Our first goal achieved, I dispatch Able-Seaman Kasrils ashore bearing bags of beads as earnest of our good intentions.

17h00. Judging from activity around large three-legged pot on beach our Able-Seaman is now Consommé Kasrils. Time to get tough. Semaphore invitation to tea.

Monday 08h30. Two canoes approach. We fire one-gun salute, splintering last remaining lifeboat.

19h15. Two rival chiefs board, wearing diamond-studded bones through their noses. Must be hell to sneeze.

20h15. Chiefs refuse peace pipe on grounds smoking endangers health. I lose my temper and order them taken below to see what an advanced civilisation can do with industrial solvent. They fall on their knees in worship before our gibbering Captain.

21h00. Transpires chiefs are high priests of cargo cult which believes god will manifest himself in the form of a midget frothing at the mouth. Traded Captain for glass beads. They also threw in slightly parboiled, inedible Able-Seaman Kasrils who is labouring under the misapprehension he is someone called Kurtz.

23h00. Mission accomplished. Peace in our time. Set course for home.

24h00. Lost at sea. Surrounded by over-size ice cubes. Anyone finding this paper in a bottle please convey the following message to the President's Office, Cape Town: ANYBODY THERE? HELP!

Lord Nelson

May 9 1997

Office of the President

Dear Walter,

The aliens have landed! I was lying in bed at Libertas late on Saturday morning, mentally rehearsing a speech to Her Majesty the Queen for delivery when I meet her this week – commiserating with her imminent loss of a son, but consoling her with the thought that she will be gaining a Rottweiler – when I heard a loud bang outside.

Rushing to the window I saw, sitting in the middle of the lawn, what looked like a small microwave oven. Hurriedly I summoned our intelligence chief, Joe Nhlanhla, who became very excited, frantically signalling that it was a temporary sojourner from Mars come to discover whether there was intelligent life on earth.

After a hurried consultation with my aides it was decided that the alien should be treated like any other foreign dignitary. Accordingly I marched out and, after a welcoming speech in which I made reference to the parlous state of the African National Congress's finances, draped the Good Hope Medal (gold) over it. To my alarm the door of the microwave oven swung open, the medal was sucked inside and the door banged shut again. Munching noises were followed by squawking and the machine rolled on to its back, little wheels spinning in the air before it fell still.

Fearing it had died of lead poisoning, I had Parks hurriedly digging a grave under a rhododendron bush when the machine appeared to recover, shakily righting itself.

Reasoning that our job was to impress it as to the intelligence of terrestrial life, I called for a copy of *The Star* and presented it to the machine. It duly swallowed the newspaper then let out a series of explosions which seemed to betoken an extreme case of flatulence.

Suddenly it trundled off the lawn and headed down the road to the Union Buildings, heading unerringly for the Department of Foreign Affairs and into the office of the minister, who was snoring contentedly behind his desk. With various probes which it telescoped out of its body the machine prodded and poked at Nzo before trundling off again, making buzzing noises. Parks whispered to me that the machine appeared to be transmitting radio signals to its control centre on Mars. Cryptographers at the National Intelligence Agency (NIA) were frantically working to decode them.

The machine, meanwhile, went trundling down the road again, heading for Johannesburg. On its way it survived two hijack bids and an AK-47 broadside from a member of the Long Distance Taxi Association who suspected the machine was trying to muscle in on his route.

Somewhat battered it rolled up at the gates of Ellis Park where a drunken hawker presented it with a can of Lion Lager. After consuming it the machine swelled to an alarming degree. Several burps were followed by the partial collapse of its undercarriage. Blowing plastic bubbles from an exhaust pipe it weaved its way to the stands.

Watching 30 grown men beating one another up while pursuing a pig's bladder around the field, the buzzing from the machine built up to a crescendo as the final whistle sounded. Just then Parks rushed up to me with an envelope, gasping that the NIA had decoded the radio transmissions.

Solemnly I opened it and read the first communication from a Martian read by mankind.

"For Chrissake, beam me up, Scotty."

Nelson
July 11 1997

View from the gallery 1

Mungo Soggot

South Africa's Acting President, Mangosuthu Buthelezi, could not restrain himself. He had spent two hours watching a string of politicians do the Masakhane, with speeches full of pledges and snipes. By then, most of the Cabinet ministers had skulked off, leaving a lonely Minister of Provincial Affairs and Constitutional Development Valli Moosa to give the Cabinet's imprimatur to Masakhane Focus Week.

"Do you have any information where the other ministers are?" the acting president beamed. "I will need to give a complete report to the president."

Moosa replied that many of his colleagues were in Lausanne, Switzerland, supporting Cape Town's Olympic bid. "And the rest who were here earlier?" inquired Buthelezi. Moosa suggested several other ministers were bound for the Southern African Development Community conference in Blantyre.

"With respect, those going to Malawi left this morning," countered the acting president. Moosa's quiver was empty, but he conceded graciously: "Other members who are neither in Malawi nor Switzerland are not here because, I am convinced, of their commitment to implementing Masakhane."

Earlier that afternoon, the Masakhane Focus Week festivities had started off with a low-key photo opportunity for Moosa and other MPs. They had all signed glossy Masakhane pledge forms which were circulated through Parliament and which even committed parliamentarians to paying their traffic fines. Most of the fun ended there.

Local government guru Pravin Gordhan fired the starting pistol for political point-scoring. He lashed out at the Democratic Party and the National Party for failing to encourage their affluent constituents to pay up. "Opposition parties have become a euphemism for undermining the RDP [Reconstruction and Development Programme]," he suggested, before asking all parties to stand together in support of Masakhane.

The DP's Douglas Gibson said the DP fully supported the campaign. "The culture of entitlement is the saboteur of efforts to build our economy." He gave a quick résumé of South Africa's dazzling service arrears figures, which leapt from R439-million to R5,5-billion between 1994 and 1996. This, he said, had been attributed to better record-keeping in local governments across the country, adding: "I can only hope that record-keeping doesn't improve further."

The Pan African Congress was a touch more controversial. After blaming the ANC for nurturing a culture of non-payment while it was a liberation movement, Mike Muendane triggered a small riot when he said of the majority party: "Coming to the crime levels, is it not the same liberation movement that is now in power that used hijackers and drug traffickers in their logistics during the struggle days?"

One of the few Cabinet ministers present, Tito Mboweni, leapt from his seat for the nearest microphone. He interrupted Muendane's scathing précis of the ANC's tactics in the constitutional negotiations to invite the PAC MP to name these drug traffickers.

Muendane retorted: "Why should I name them when you know them?" This triggered a raucous exchange which was cut short by the deputy speaker.

The African Christian Democratic Party did not take a snipe at any of its political opponents, but could not resist a plug for the Bible and its teaching that "when you die you leave everything behind".

September 5 1997

View from the gallery 2

Marion Edmunds and Mungo Soggot

FW de Klerk took the podium in Parliament this week to deliver a speech marking his departure, but the swansong degenerated into an ugly shouting match between the African National Congress and his supporters.

In the din, De Klerk probably failed to notice some of the subtler gestures of appreciation from former Cabinet opponents. Minister of Health Nkosazana Zuma clapped cautiously as the former president rose, but stopped when booing erupted in the ANC backbench.

De Klerk thanked those who had supported him in his long political career. "For me this is a poignant moment," he said. The statement was greeted with jeers and laughter. Minister of Labour Tito Mboweni shifted uneasily in his seat, and shot disapproving looks at the members' benches. Nor did any of his ANC Cabinet colleagues participate in the heckling. Most looked down, faces serious and arms folded.

De Klerk tried hard to squeeze a little sympathy from the crowd. "Memories come flooding back. It was from this podium that I announced the release of President Nelson Mandela and the unbanning of the ANC," said De Klerk. The ANC booed.

De Klerk drew in a deep breath, to shout out his next sentence: "What I won't miss is the lack of manners of a few members in the back benches," he eventually retorted. *"Foeitog!"* they shouted back.

But the ANC was not the only voice in the chamber. The public gallery just above was packed with enthusiastic NP supporters – and a strong Cape Flats contingent – who had travelled to Parliament to hail the new NP leader. They took on the ANC from above, boo for boo, and cheered boisterously at anything that De Klerk said. The National Assembly began to sound like a soccer pitch.

"Point of order, point of order," yelled an ANC member in a splendid red jersey. "Is it acceptable that the public gallery clap when members make speeches?"

At the start of his speech, De Klerk had thanked the Speaker, Frene Ginwala, for providing much-needed protection from his opposition during his time in Parliament. Now she was in a corner.

"Order! Order!" she shouted and explained that the new rules permitted the public gallery to clap. However, "the members of the public gallery should not behave in such a way that does not enhance debate", she added.

"On behalf of my supporters I promise we won't dance in Parliament," shouted De Klerk, no doubt referring to the toyi-toyi, to which he has been subjected in the past. The public gallery went wild with delight; the back-benchers scowled, quiet for a moment.

Smug from that small triumph, De Klerk went on. "I miss the cut-and-thrust of the incisive debate which we used to have," he lectured. "And I hope for the sake of South Africa that the young parliamentarians will find ways and means to restore a culture of constructive, lively debate."

His victory was short-lived. The booing erupted again. He wound things up, and left the podium. So it was that the man who had once commanded near-control of Parliament, albeit one of a different stripe, was drowned out by the majority voice.

September 12 1997

View from the gallery 3
Marion Edmunds

The man who won the hearts of the African National Congress this week was backbench Eastern Cape MP Mbulelo Goniwe, who targeted Democratic Party leader Tony Leon in a scathing attack.

Taking the podium, in the debate on President Nelson Mandela's opening of Parliament speech, Goniwe started in a loud voice: "We have just endured a typical Tony Leon tirade ... Mr Leon has pretensions of being the moral conscience of South Africa ... But Mr Leon's holier-than-thou posturing is intended to shift attention from his party's failings to the imagined failings of our government."

The ANC backbenchers loved it. "Yes!" they shouted in chorus.

Leon sat listening, his head characteristically cocked upwards, nose in the air and a little to the side, now and then purposefully folding up pieces of paper to place in his inside pocket or the bin.

"Does the DP think our memory is so short? We have not forgotten that while our president was breaking rocks on Robben Island, the Progressive Party wished to reserve the vote only for those with property or education," shouted Goniwe.

"Yes!" shouted the ANC backbenchers, and even Cabinet members were smiling now, while Mandela looked on, poker-faced. Leon, only minutes before, had accused Mandela of leading the ANC down a populist blind alley.

Mandela had looked on with the same poker face as Leon exclaimed: "The depiction of opponents of the ANC as racist enemies of transformation,

Stent

determined to sabotage our fragile democratic order, is a sinister attempt to stifle dissent and distort debate.

"It is a sort of political fundamentalism which proclaims: 'I'm right, you're wrong, go to hell!'" he insisted, while the backbenchers heckled.

His force was in marked contrast to IFP leader Mangosuthu Buthelezi's grace. In a gentle, congratulatory speech, Buthelezi had addressed the same theme.

"Personally," he said, stumbling slightly over his words, "I do not think anyone in this house is an enemy of the people ... We must accept that the interests of the South African people are diversified and all are duly entitled to be heard and represented without being lambasted."

But now Goniwe was on the podium: "We have not forgotten that Mr Leon leads a party which supported conscription into a white army, which was sent to kill our children in the townships and eliminate the freedom fighters of Southern Africa."

Limpho Hani, wife of the late Chris Hani, was almost weeping with delirious joy, gesticulating at Leon.

"Is it any wonder that the good burghers of Boksburg and Roodepoort, home of conservatism, are now flocking to the DP? They have found a new spiritual home ..."

Even sleepy Minister of Foreign Affairs Alfred Nzo perked up to smile at the DP leader. It was Leon's turn to be poker-faced.

Goniwe climaxed: "Next year, Mr Leon will stand before this house. The world will be coming to an end. Only Tony Leon will be able to see it, only Tony Leon will be able to save it. What arrogance!"

He swept off the podium and walked to Mandela, who shook his hand, his sombre, tired face breaking into a warm Madiba smile, before Goniwe returned to the hugs and handshakes of the party faithful.

February 13 1998

View from the gallery 4

Mungo Soggot

South Africa's street-activist-turned-minister-of-finance effortlessly cruised through his second budget this week, delivering the bad news with wit and the good news with his trademark Cheshire-cat grin.

It was a virtuoso performance by Trevor Manuel – except for the blaps at the end when he thanked President Nelson Mandela "in his absence" for his support. Mandela had been there from the start sipping Perrier water and absorbing how his finance minister intends walking the tightrope of a low-growth, pre-election economy.

Manuel swiftly reminded the house how last year the president had prompted him when he lost his place, but that this time he had been so silent. "My sincerest apologies," he offered to Mandela and to guffawing parliamentarians.

Manuel could be excused for missing the president, having had to contend for the past hour with not only two teleprompters – hopelessly camouflaged by some plants - but also a written text on the lectern before him.

"We must root out corruption, which eats at the fabric of society. For that reason we must do everything in our power to uproot it in government and business," Manuel said in halting Sesotho during his opening remarks. There were cheers from the ruling party and a few giggles from all, including Deputy President Thabo Mbeki, as Manuel wrestled with the vernacular.

Manuel gave special mentions only to Minister of Labour Tito Mboweni – for his successful labour-relations strategy – and, for less obvious reasons, to Minister of Housing Sankie Mthembi-Mahanyele, who applauded herself as Manuel celebrated her achievements in the housing field.

Minister of Water Affairs and Forestry Kader Asmal was the most demonstrative in his approbation for the individual department allocations, giving a small whistle of excitement when Manuel announced a hike in education spending to R6,5-billion.

Asmal, as is now the custom, took centre stage when Manuel turned to "sin taxes" and expressly apologised to the water minister as he announced hefty increases in cigarette tax. "Tax on cigarettes, Professor Asmal, will go up by 29%."

Thabo Mbeki got off more lightly, with pipe tobacco going up an average of only R2,11/kg. Communications minister Jay Naidoo was the only minister who applauded as Manuel announced increases in tax on liquor – except for sorghum beer "because of the howls of disapproval last year from Dr [Mangosuthu] Buthelezi when I announced the charge on sorghum beer".

Manuel's colleagues giggled wryly when he announced his surprise decision to hit South Africa's recently demutualised life assurers with a special tax.

Manuel explained how he had called in the heads of Old Mutual and Sanlam to announce the move that morning. "I want to express my appreciation for the manner in which they received the news."

The minister was effusive in his praise for his team at the Ministry of Finance, led by his trusted lieutenant, Maria Ramos. "They have given up time and sleep – both theirs and mine," he said, before lapping up a standing ovation.

Manuel's mother, seated alongside Govan Mbeki, looked on admiringly as the ruling party filed out in a glow of self-congratulation. The opposition, meanwhile, sharpened its knives over what Democratic Party chief Tony Leon, momentarily unsure of his constituency, branded a budget that was "bad for the poor, the unemployed and the motorist".

March 13 1998

If Mobutu were to come back ...
Cameron Duodu

I wonder whether Congolese politicians realise the impatience and irritation with which the rest of us in Africa look on as they squabble over the terms of the peace agreement that could give their country a chance to recover from the ravages of Mobutu Sese Seko's kleptocratic rule?

Don't the Congolese politicians have any sense of history at all? Mobutu used to boast, with Gaullist aplomb: *"Aprés moi le deluge!"*

Yet the ambition of the Congolese politicians to obtain power for themselves has blinded them to the irony of their proving Mobutu right. Nothing that they have done since his death two years ago reveals that they have the slightest interest in bringing peace to their country. Yet without peace, they cannot give the Congolese people a chance to rebuild their lives and repair their devastated country.

Angered by the meandering posturing of these heads-of-state-in-waiting (one could pick 20 of them out of a hat, just like that) I sought permission to interview Mobutu.

The Big Boss agreed, but Mobutu said he would only come down if I brought President Laurent Kabila, and rebel leaders Abdoulaye Ndombasi, Jean-Pierre Ondekane, Ernest Wamba-dia-Wamba, Emile Ilunga, Bizima Karaha, Lunda Bululu and Jean-Pierre Bemba before him. The Big Boss agreed to lend me temporary powers that would enable me to bring all of them together.

I now fully understand the frustration of former president Nelson Mandela and others who have sought to get the Congolese leaders to agree on a peace settlement.

Here is the unedited transcript:

Mobutu: You, Kabila, what sort of Congolese are you? You are selling the Congo's mineral resources to the Zimbabweans.

Kabila: You've been dead for two years and when you come back, the first thing you worry about is money? Listen to who is talking!

Didn't you sell our mineral rights to the Americans and the Belgians? Did you keep the money in Africa?

Bululu: So you admit you are giving contracts to the Zimbabweans?

Kabila: Do you think their aeroplanes drink water?

Wamba: That is why you didn't want an elected Parliament, isn't it? You knew they would ask you to bring all contracts before Parliament for ratification.

Ndombasi: Shut up! Didn't you send people to Unita's Jonas Savimbi to find out how you could sell diamonds without paying duty on them?

Ilunga: Gentlemen, gentlemen! Remember in whose presence you are! You may think he's dead, but there's always blood in the head of a tsetse fly.

Karaha: We are all Congolese.

Kabila: Listen to that Tutsi calling himself a Congolese!

Mobutu: So this is what you have sunk down to? After all the lessons in Congolese nationalism and *authenticité* that I taught you?

Ilunga: Ha ha ha ha! You only taught each of us to build a Gbadolite for himself, *monsieur le président*! Kabila has already put in papers to grab your apartments in the most fashionable areas of Paris and Brussels. All in the name of the Congolese people, of course.

Bululu: Some of us learned your lessons better than others, *monsieur le président*.

Mobutu: Hmm! I know where you guys are coming from. I know. If only I could have had a little more time, I would have settled all your problems. Remember what I did for Nguza Karl i-Bond?

Kabila: Who wants to be sentenced to death only to be released with fanfare and made a rich man?

Mobutu: That is reconciliation, man, reconciliation. You, Kabila, you have these problems because you are so headstrong.

Karaha: Your excellency, Kabila doesn't like people to make comments about the size of his head. If you want a serious conversation with him, please don't.

Mobutu: We Congolese are always too serious about ourselves, that's the trouble. We have good music, we have the most beautiful women, but we always leave them and fight about politics.

Bululu: Or we fight about politics so that we can have the power to bend the musicians and the ladies to our will, not so, the Cock-who-doesn't-allow-the-hens-to-sleep-at-night? Who imprisoned Rochero, eh? Who turned Franco into a silly crooner who sang the Belgian national anthem on board a ship at a reception for the king of Belgium, eh?

Mobutu: You Congolese never forget anything. Nor do you learn anything.

Kabila: You are damned right. You think you can come here and lecture us about what is good for Congo when you took 30 years ruining it?

Mobutu: So you too want 30 years to do the same, do you?

Wamba: As a person who tries to bring a historical perspective to discussions, I have to point out that this discussion would have been more to the point if you had sought permission to bring Patrice Lumumba with you. Then he could have posed questions to you too.

Ilunga: What about Tshombe? Moise Tshombe? You don't think he could have had something to teach us about the Congo? Was it not he who showed us that the country could be carved up into little parts supported by outside powers?

Ndombasi: If we are going to stake out claims for past leaders, then I don't think Cyril Adoula should be left out!

Karaha: Nor Kasavubu!

Wamba: Nor Kamitatu!

Kabila: Nor Soumialot!

Ndombasi: Nor Gizenga!

(At the mention of each name, there are opposing shouts of "Yeah!", "No!", "Traitor!", "Patriot!", "Sell-out!", "Victorious leader!", "Quisling!", "Hero!", "Sissy!", until finally pandemonium breaks out.)

Big Boss: Time, gentlemen, please. No last orders!

Exeunt severally. Curtain.

July 2 1999

Barney subpoenas God
David Beresford

It was at 6.30am that Barney awoke, to the cock-o-doodle-doo of a hahdedah playing silly buggers in the garden. He stifled the impulse to hurl the Tea'sMade out the window. To cure him of the habit Leonora the maid had attached a rubber band. The last time he had done himself a serious injury.

Barney winced at the memory of the pain. Sinking back into the comfort of his pillow, he winced again as the memory collided with the immediacy of the pain and inwardly groaned as his mind hastily began rifling through his memories of the night before.

They had worked into the early hours of the morning as usual, first agonising judiciously over the weighty complaints from the Pink Lawyer's Association and the Association of Pink Accountants. Then they had turned to the press.

It was Moodley's brainwave that had started the rot. It seemed to be inspired at the time; an idea whose time had finally come. "We'll shut the whole bang-shoot up by subpoenaing the lot of them," his legal adviser had declared, excitedly leaping from one foot to the other. "We'll sub-judice them all, rat-a-tat-a-tat-a-tat," he shouted as he sprayed the imaginary editors, newspaper proprietors and other forms of thieving, murdering, stinking, racist, garbage, journalistic low-life with his imaginary AK-47.

When they had dealt with all the South African editors with the help of sealing wax, quill pen and Barney's priceless 1964 edition of the *Guide to the Gothic in Calligraphy*, the question was what to do with the foreigners. "No problem," Moodley declared with the sang-froid of a man who had peered at a thousand menacing hordes from behind the ramparts of Butterfield's *DIY Guide to Delict, Summonses and Subpoenas*. He then rushed off in search of the *International Guide to the Media*.

The pile of subpoenas to melanin-deprived editors around the globe had nearly reached the ceiling when someone raised the question of the Great Editor in the Sky.

"If they have nothing to hide ..." suggested Claudia, hesitatingly.

"Nobody can be beyond the reach ..." offered Moodley.

"We owe it to the past ..." added Barney.

They all nodded solemnly. The historic decision taken, Moodley explained that it would count as due service if they made reasonable efforts to bring the subpoena to His attention. "Or Hers," he added hurriedly as the beam in Claudia's hand began swinging ominously in his direction.

Quoting various authorities regarding the presumptions of omniscience on the part of the Almighty, he assured them it would satisfy the courts to affix it to the nearest steeple, dome, bell tower or other such protuberance.

Glumly Barney shook his head. Still fresh in his mind was the sight of a local evangelist, Ray "Mr Universe" McCauley's already over-inflated chest further inflated by a flak jacket after the national cricket team had taken it upon themselves to vote him chaplain-in-chief. "Religious war," he muttered dismissively. The mayhem which would ensue if he hazarded a guess as to up whose chimney God was to be found!

He sat bolt upright. "Got it," he cried! "The Constitution. It's non-sectarian ... where's the ladder?" he shouted over his shoulder as he led them racing down the stairs.

"The garden shed!" shouted back Moodley as they burst into the night air and hurried across the moonlit lawn.

"Oww!" shouted Claudia hopping painfully, if gracefully, behind the excited pack after she had collided with an unseen concrete object.

"*Les nains du jardin ont aussi des droits* [Garden gnomes have rights too]!" shouted one such of French manufacture, indignantly fishing around in the shrubbery for his concrete beret.

"*Allez-vous faire foutre,*"* rejoined the indignant girl after a brief pause to consider the constitutional position.

Barney tottered out of the dark under the weight of a ladder, Moodley

* "Fuck off."

close behind clutching a box of nails and a hammer. Together they made their way to the flagpole standing proudly in front of their offices. Clambering to the top, Barney pulled a sheet of paper out of his breast pocket and hammered it into the top of the pole.

"Three cheers for the chief!" shouted Moodley below. "Hip, hip ..."

He got no further. Out of a seemingly cloudless sky came an almighty clap of thunder accompanying a bolt of lightning which whizzed between Barney's legs, driving a 1,8m-deep crater into the ground.

On top of the pole Barney froze, gazing upwards at a brilliant burning and spinning ball of light which had materialised about 6m above his head.

"What's this?" bellowed a Voice from the said ball. A sudden gust of wind ripped the subpoena off the flagpole and zipped it into the flames. "Rights! Human rights! I'm the only one with rights around here," the Voice raged. There was a rummaging sound followed by the irritated mutter: "Now where have I put those sodding things, oh for Christ ..."

"It's only an invitation!" hurriedly explained Barney. "Followed by some entirely hypothetical stuff about imprisonment ..."

"Not another religion, is it?" peevishly interrupted the Voice, having apparently abandoned the eternal search for his glasses.

"No no, no ... ""

"So?"

"Ehhh. Are you a subliminal?" inquired Barney automatically.

"I don't know," the brilliant burning ball replied, a defensive edge of uncertainty entering his voice.

"Well, you wouldn't, would you, stupid!" snapped Barney.

A second bolt of lightning flashed between his legs. His aides, forgotten down below, dived for cover behind an all-white rubbish bin.

"Ahem ... well, are you previously disadvantaged?" asked Barney, hastily re-assuming an obsequious posture.

"Not really," replied the burning ball, sounding puzzled.

"Have you ever undergone the pencil test?" Barney inquired, trying another tack.

"Pencil test?" echoed the Voice, the burning, spinning ball roiling in a threateningly muscular sort of a way.

"Can I see you?" bleated Barney, the tension proving too much. His stomach lurched and he closed his eyes, bracing himself for the third lightning blast, remembering too late that looking at Him (or Her) was a strict no-no.

"Oh sure. Funny, no one else ever asked that before," said the Voice gaily.

Cautiously Barney opened his eyes. To his astonishment a figure was sharing the top rung of the ladder with him. He gaped as he took in the outline, the colour ...

"Hello, ducky," said the apparition, coyly cocking a wrist.

Yes God was ...

At this precise moment Barney awoke to the cock-o-doodle-doo of a distant cockerel whose bedside digital clock needed a new battery. "The tea will be cold," he thought in dismay, glancing at his watch.

February 25 2000

Part Five
Cultural Weapons

Porn or art, there were no tickets to Tango
Arthur Goldstuck, Mike Sarakinsky and Jeff Zerbst

Outside, the rain washes the grime of the city away to lay bare the sleaze of the night. The words of the prophets are written on the noticeboard: "Sold Out".

Hundreds of people in raincoats (it was raining) with hats pulled down over murky faces are skulking around the entrance to the Seven Arts Cinema in Norwood. We are there to record a little bit of history, because this is the first South African public screening of Bernardo Bertolucci's *Last Tango in Paris*.

There is excitement in the air, along with frustrated anger as would-be patrons are turned away. Black market tickets are reputedly going for R50, but they're all too few; the idea is to get inside, not to take the money and run.

Ticketless, we took a camera, a tape recorder and a notebook to the patrons to capture the moment and to find out if they were there for the art or the porn. No one came clean ...

Enter Jennifer Yuill and Dean Slotar.

Reporters: Are you here for the art or the porn?

Jennifer: If I want to see porn I can do it. I don't have to watch other people doing it. Really. I'm a student of film. I'm looking at it from that point of view.

Dean: Censorship sucks.

Derek Bauer's World

Derek Bauer

Enter John Ferreira and Carla Voigt. They're both "in the business".

John: I feel that my education, and I mean that in the true sense of the word, is not complete if I haven't seen this. It runs for two hours and I would gladly have stood at the back to watch. I think the people who are here tonight are all movie buffs because this is a movie-buff house. I don't think people are here for the sensationalism, they're here to see a true work of art. It's a pity people misconstrue that, because it's a cult movie. I think one just has to see it, it's something that, if you're a movie buff, you just have to see. It's Bertolucci. It's Brando. It's a marvellous film, you've just go to see it. It's a great work of art.

Reporters: Don't you think our censorship laws have contributed towards a sense of sensationalism?

John: No, I think that the laws are far more enlightened than in many countries. I can, for instance, tell you that a lot of violent films that have passed uncut in South Africa have been heavily cut or restricted in places like Sweden, and in Latin America a lot of dialogue is cut ...

Carla: Censorship in this country has gone forward in leaps and bounds. Unfortunately the public is very unaware of it.

Enter a Rastafarian who preferred to keep his name to himself.

Reporters: Why have you come to see the film?

Rasta: A bra told me this film was playing and it was banned.

Reporters: Are you here out of curiosity to see what sort of thing is getting past the censors?

Rasta: No.

Reporters: Do you know what the movie's about?

Rasta: I don't even know what it's called, bra. Hey bra, no photo.

Enter Chris Fourie.

Reporters: What are you expecting to see?

Chris: Well, I dunno.

Reporters: What have you heard about it?

Chris: Just that it was banned, like that other one, what was it called ... *Clockwork Orange.*

Reporters: Do you think this is an art movie or a blue movie?

Chris: No, I don't think this is a blue movie. I have seen blue movies and I mean I wouldn't have come here if I thought this was a blue movie. It's not my scene.

Reporters: Do you know who the director is?

Chris: No.

Reporters: But you know who's in it – some of the stars?

Chris: Ag, names I'm very bad at. Numbers you can ask me.

Enter John Geleta.

Reporters: What would you have paid for a black market ticket, sir?

John: I wouldn't have paid. I'm cynical enough to believe that it will show again, that this one-off's just to make sure there's a full house. I believe it will show again quite a few times before the end of the year.

Enter a long line of patrons. Theo Pampallis leaps out.

Theo: I feel pretty strongly about this. I don't think it should have been advertised on Radio Highveld. You've probably got all the raincoat brigade here. I have an uncle who listens to Highveld and I heard this thing coming over the air. I think it should just have stayed internal, within the festival-goers, then we would have got people who wanted to see it because it was a Bertolucci movie.

When the bell rung its final call to the faithful to take their seats, we went to talk to Len Davis of Festival Films, the man responsible for organising the screening.

Reporters: Do you see this as a bit of a coup?

Davis: I don't know. I mean, we've managed to show *The Life of Brian*, and in the South African historical sense, that was more of a coup.

Reporters: What are the chances of seeing *Last Tango* again?

Davis: I think it'll be submitted again in a year or two by the distributors, so it's up to them. We've been given permission to show it once.

Reporters: How about some tickets?

Davis: Sure, go in and talk to Brando. Get the inside story.

Enter Brando, wiping butter off his hands, mumbling incoherently in French.

Reporters: Marlon, what do you think of all this fuss?

Brando: Call me Paul, but not in this apartment. We have no names in here, remember. I've been thinking some things through, and this is my message to a changing South Africa: "You're alone, you're all alone and you won't be able to be free of that feeling of being alone until you look death right in the face. I mean, that sounds like cinematic bullshit, until you go right up into the ass of death, right up into its ass, until you find a womb of fear, or the residue of last night's butter." See you guys. Your two hours are up.

Reporters: So long, Paul, er, Marlon, er, Mister. But before you go, tell us, please. Was it art?

Brando: What kind of critics are you? Didn't you notice the Italian director, the French dialogue mixed with English? The film within the film, the long shots, the close-ups, the soft focus, the subtitles? The setting in the poor quarters of Paris, the non-sequiturs, sex with clothes on, sex with clothes off, sex in the bath, the razor blade, squabbling over a burial? The Freudian metaphors, the Jungian influences? And not forgetting the tango competition. Wasn't I great?

Reporters: Terrific ass. Now tell us what you really think. Was it art?

Brando: Ask the guy in the third row with the raincoat.

October 23 1987

Tale of some teeth

Krisjan Lemmer

You know, some of you out there are simply not going to believe the story I am about to tell you. And I don't blame you for a minute.

The scene is the not-so-shabby Zoo Lake restaurant in Johannesburg. In steps Catherine Deneuve – the one in the movies is the fake – accompanied by, and I say this with sorrow, a typical Jo'burg male. We're talking white suit here, red shirt, white shoes, gold chain nestling on bounteous chest wig.

The man sits back looking smug, watching everyone watching Deneuve, and then the waiter arrives and says a few words. Chest-wig looks livid: "What do you mean? What's wrong with my teeth?" The waiter tries again. "That's it. We're leaving right now," bellows white suit, and storms out with the gal in tow.

A fellow diner calls the ashen-faced waiter over. What was that all about? "I don't know. I just asked him if he wanted an aperitif."

April 5 1990

Film shot down in SA, but soars abroad

Ivor Powell

Last Tuesday, there was a special screening of the film *Shot Down*. Friends, crew members, a few bemused relatives and a representative sample of the Johannesburg demi-monde in general, turned out at the Halfway House cinema for what may well prove its one and only public screening in South Africa.

Some time earlier *Shot Down* was submitted by the Durban Film Festival for consideration to the Publications Control Board. It was banned on Thursday.

Oh, yes, and director Andrew Worsdale, veteran of the Weekend Theatre group, was awarded his master's degree from UCLA on the same day.

It's not really surprising that it should have been banned. Among other things, it features excerpts from Matthew Krouse and Robert Colman's *Famous Dead Man* which, if you remember, was decidedly not the kind of memorial Betsie Verwoerd was after for her famous dead husband – and a pornographic sequence entitled *Die Voortrekkers*. This, by the way, is a sequence where Worsdale chooses to do a Hitchcock and make his cameo appearance. The film also featured assorted blasphemies and obscenities.

"I think it would be fair to say *Shot Down* was motivated by disgust more than by anything else," Jeremy Nathan, the film's producer, says, looking owlish. "You go to the movies and you look at the audience. You hate and detest these people, you know ... I mean, how do you make a movie feeling like that?"

Life being what it is, as somebody – Victor Hugo, I think – once said, one seeks revenge. Out of that desire for revenge and out of a kind of self-loathing peculiar to white South Africans, you create a character like Paul Gilliat, that's what you do. And you put him into an average jol on an average night in Jo'burg ...

Gilliat: government spy, consummate slob, whingeing hypocrite continually mistaking self-pity for existential crisis, is a thoroughly unlikable character. He is what, to emulate the film's literary style, one might call a turd squeezed from the bowels of everything that is monstrous in the system. At the same time, it's hard not to recognise something of oneself in him.

"To put our state of mind into the cinema was more important than the story," Worsdale says. "That's why we wrote around things that were happening at the time ... *Famous Dead Man*, the spray-painting by right-wing thugs of the Black Sun the day before an End Conscription Campaign concert was supposed to happen ... all those things.

"In the first draft, Gilliat was a lefty ... quite a sympathetic character," he goes on.

"But as shooting progressed I pushed Robert [Colman] to deliver more and more of an obnoxious, egocentric performance ... We used to marvel at how horrible he was ... When we were shooting in the final sequences, everybody was on set saying let's kill him, let's kill him ..."

It is definitely one of the strengths of the film, and a locus of its authenticity, that Gilliat and everything around him is so rotten. But it also raises a whole lot of questions. I mean, how do a group of people who have never made a film before, who rest on little more than the rather ragged laurels of Weekend Theatre, get the money to make something like that?

"Tax dodge," says Nathan happily.

But the backers, what did they think of the script?

"They didn't even want to read the script. Not interested. We don't even know who they are ... We suspect they may be rightwingers, but it makes no difference, it's a purely financial thing."

The truth of it is that, under the old tax laws, the film doesn't even have to get shown to make money for its backers.

Well, *Shot Down* went on to win the Special Prize – awarded by the festival itself, rather than the judges, at last year's Mannheim festival. It received an invitation to show at Brussels's prestigious L'Age d'Or festival, was shown to some acclaim at CASA in Amsterdam and is the focus of some interest at the ICA in London and Channel Four television in Britain. So they shouldn't really be complaining.

But they still haven't made any money back on the film. The Publications Board may well have solved that problem though. There's nothing that provokes foreign interest half so quickly as foolish banning.

March 4 1988

Dr. Jack

Shit-collecting

Krisjan Lemmer

You know the other day I was sitting in the Dorsbult Bar with a few of my gabbas, with nothing to do. Anyway, up on the box comes this my favourite ad about Blue Ribbon Bread – the one with the men from the bakery delivering the fresh bread at the crack of dawn and this lovely liedjie which goes "*teza mlongwe, teza mlongwe*". But ou Hennie van Winkel, who hasn't forgotten any of his mine-days fanagalo, just smiles: "Ja, it's a pretty picture, but somebody should have told them that *teza mlongwe* means 'to collect the shit'."

July 26 1991

Elvis is alive ... in Turffontein

Charlotte Bauer and John Perlman

The dance floor is full, the lights are low and Elvis Presley is giving *There Goes My Everything* all that he's got. Suddenly the King steps forward, unwinds a silk scarf from around his neck and hands it to the woman closest to the stage. She gasps, screams, then covers her rubbed-red eyes. The song winds down and Elvis, splendid in a glittering blue suit, speaks: "*Baie dankie. Ek wil julle baie graag aan my band voorstel. Dames en here, Die Cadillacs ...*"

This ain't Las Vegas, ladies and gents. This is Turffontein – the Southern Country restaurant to be precise, a wide and warm south Jo'burg club where the drafts are deep, the portions big and the waitresses say "Don't drink from this" as they bring you a finger bowl.

Throughout August, Elvis Presley fans – real Elvis Presley fans – have been getting together to listen to the music, dance the dances and swap souvenirs. But tonight is the big one – this is the day the King died.

That was 13 years ago, of course, but Elsa Nell, secretary of the Official Elvis Presley Fan Club of South Africa, still took the week off her job as a receptionist at Eskom "to mourn Elvis properly. I spend the time listening to his music and watching his videos," she said. "This morning I woke up crying and when I go home tonight I will cry myself to sleep."

Nell is wearing an Elvis sweatshirt and an Elvis watch. She says she first heard the King when she saw *GI Blues* "at the old Clarendon bioscope. I was 10 at the time and I just started yelling. He was magic, just magic and there could never be two Elvises. That is why his twin brother had to die at birth."

Nell has little time for any other musicians. "Jerry Lee Lewis is one guy who could maybe give him a run for his money, but not the others. Cliff Richard was a real *klooster koek*. But my absolute worst is Iron Maiden."

And she still clings to a hope that Elvis is still alive. "Somebody like Elvis could never die. I like to think that he is busy making a video. When he really dies they will release it and it will tell the whole story of what he has been doing all these years."

Nell is saving up to visit Graceland, the King's Memphis home, next year. But she can't imagine what it would have been like to meet him. "I wouldn't have got anywhere near Elvis because I would have fainted. I might even have died. He was a real ladies' man," she says.

"He was a man's man," says Tony Wolfaardt, proprietor of the Southern Country and president of the club. Wolfaardt doesn't expect to see Elvis again. "He's a goner," he says. For him, remembering Elvis is also about recalling his own youth, a time when teenage was starting to mean more than just older than 12 but not yet 20.

"In those days when we used to smoke pot it wasn't because we were trying to be cool, it was because we were trying to be bad. But jeez, you know, you could still spend hours at a roadhouse on just two milkshakes, car-hopping and chatting up the chicks," he says.

"Apartheid was another funny thing in those days too, you know. We all used to go to the Zoo Lake in our stovepipes, and we would get up on tea boxes and play pennywhistles with the black guys there. I can't even remember when apartheid moved in."

"The Elvis thing is going to get bigger and bigger," Wolfaardt says. "Right now, he is still the fifth-highest-paid entertainer in the world. Elvis has become a corporation."

One man helping to keep that corporation going is Hannes Nell, Elsa's husband. "If I see something in a shop about Elvis and I don't buy it, all hell breaks loose if Elsa finds out," Nell says. "Elvis made 836 songs and she has about 500 of them. And the house is full of books about Elvis – mind you, she has just as many books about Hitler. Now he was a different kind of story, of course, but she reads as much about Hitler as she does about Elvis."

Hannes admits that his wife's obsession occasionally gets a bit much. "She was interviewed in a magazine and some guy at work said to me, 'Just look at this crazy woman. How can anybody be so mad about Elvis?' I just said ja ... I wasn't going to tell him it was my wife."

But even though he usually spends his record money on Pavarotti, he still considers himself one of the King's real fans and is keen to build up the fan club, which currently has 152 members, ranging in age from 10 to 80. The club does face one peculiarly South African difficulty. "When we phoned the club in Memphis, they told us they don't deal with South Africa. Others have said the same thing but it is starting to relax."

The first sign of the growing glasnost in the Elvis fan club world was a hefty newsletter from the Polish branch. "Of course we couldn't read it," says Hannes, "but eventually we did find someone to translate it. They say they have 25 000 members, but that one Elvis record costs them two months' wages."

The one man who seems pretty calm about all of this is Elvis himself – Nick Nel, a 25-year-old telecommunications electrician, singing for the

Nel first heard Elvis when he was a six-year-old growing up in Roodepoort. "He was singing Blue Suede Shoes and after that I kept on trying to copy the way he sang," he says.

Nel hasn't got the Elvis pelvis but the Cadillacs – three guitars and a drum machine – are tight and his voice is pretty good. A couple of nights ago it was so good that a number of women, Elsa Nell included, leapt on the stage to try and pull him off. "They tried to come in the dressing room," Nel says, but his wife – a keen Bles Bridges fan – stepped smartly in.

Elvis is still Nel's all-time favourite. "I like Roy Orbison and there have been some pretty smart bands, but nobody has had the voice. That is what gets me about Elvis." He signs autographs "Elvis – Nick Nel". But he doesn't plan to wear blue suede shoes forever.

"I have written four of my own songs and eventually I would like to make a bigger singing career for myself," he says. "I suppose you could say I am using Elvis to get somewhere.

"Sure I remember the day Elvis died. I was at school and one of my friends told me he was dead. At first I didn't believe it, but I can't say it touched me too much. I mean some day every oke has to die."

August 24 1990

Banking and brotherhood

Thami Mkhwanazi

Mxolisi mixes drinking with banking. He is able to save and receive regular lump-sum payments without having to fill in bank forms or stand in queues. In the process he downs numerous glasses of liquor with friends around him amid strains of music. He has been doing this for years every Sunday morning.

His banking method has enabled him to maintain his unemployed wife and children, his aged mother, and other members of the family. It has also helped him sustain the adverse effects of a strike now in its fourth week. He is among hundreds of workers who have downed tools at Barlows in protest against poor pay and working conditions.

He opted several years ago for membership of a stokvel savings club when it became impossible for him to support his family and furnish the four-roomed family home. Now the chairman of the Sizanani Club, Mxolisi invited me to become a "supporter" and join him at the stokvel on Sunday morning.

It was still pouring when he and I folded our umbrellas and rubbed off the mud on our shoes on the doormat in the living room at Zone 4 in Pimville.

"It's warmer this side," said Veronica, our hostess, beckoning us to the spacious dining room, where a dozen chairs were crammed around two tables put close together.

Four men smoked and chatted around a coffee table at the far end. Their voices almost drowned the music programme on the transistor radio on the coffee table.

"*Laat ons julle cook, majita* [Join us for a drink, fellows]," said one of the four, pointing at three bottles of ice-cold beer on the coffee table. It was 9.45am.

Mxolisi declined the offer. "We're okay, thanks," he said. On the main table were a dozen tumblers stacked in a tray around a bottle of Bells scotch and a bottle of Smirnoff vodka. Next to the tray stood two four-litre glass containers ("scales"), and a dozen beer quarts were placed under the table. Also adorning the table was a tot measure.

Mxolisi introduced me to our hostess, the only woman member of the 16-person club, and her family as well as other members as they trickled to their seats around the table. Each member handed him a R50 contribution before sitting down. When it is the turn of a member to host a meeting, he receives R750.

These savings don't earn any interest, but faced with a long history of deprivation, economic and otherwise, and lack of exposure to banking facilities, the availability of capital seems to be the most important thing. Sizanani is one of an estimated 800 000 stokvels.

The four "supporters" paid their contributions of R12. The fee covered liquor, coffee and brotherhood.

Most of the members had arrived and were seated by the 10am starting time. The chairman clapped his hands and ordered the radio to be turned off and everyone to be silent before he made the opening remarks. He announced a few apologies, read minutes of the last get-together and thanked everybody for attending.

He had hardly sat down when the barman opened a beer bottle with another beer bottle and quickly poured the contents into the four-litre container. "*Hamba bikiri!*" he shouted and the two "scales" on opposite sides of the table began to move from one mouth to another to the right of each drinker.

Stokvels are as much about socialising as about finance. The men discussed the Soccer City political rally on Sunday. "I don't think the Boers [government] will allow the rally to be advertised, let alone permit it," said club member Jozi.

"These guys [the government] are under heavy pressure; they may just allow it," replied Mcebisi, a supporter.

"The damn strike is killing us," said a club member, changing the subject. "*Lanies vat 'n kans* [bosses are chancers]," said another.

The barman opened the scotch and poured it into the tot measure, emptied this into a tumbler and took a swig. The glass was passed to the man on his right. He did the same with vodka, then switched back to beer.

The chairman thanked members for R140 paid towards a member's wedding that day. "I urge you all to attend the wedding afterwards," he said. More supporters arrived and made their contributions. The drinking continued and a man passed out.

The chairman stodd up again. "The spirit of the party has pleased our

Stent

hosting member, Veronica, and for that she offers a case of beer," he shouted. "Give her a big hand."

The stokvelers changed from talking to singing. At one o'clock sharp the chairman rose and sang the national anthem. Everybody joined in with fists clenched. They woke the sleeping man up and filed out of the house.

October 27 1989

She's bold but 'not beautiful'
Charlotte Bauer

We are huddled around a heater in Brenda Fassie's large office and I can't take my eyes off her slender fingers as they curl around a bottle of Beefeater gin to pour me a drink, not forgetting to slosh a good tot on to the pink plush carpet first "for the ancestors".

Her hands sparkle with the reflected warmth of a sluice of diamonds; they all belong to Fassie's wedding rings – she had wanted two sets, not one. And what Fassie wants, she usually gets, because part of the artistry of her success lies in an unerring ability to make things happen.

She shimmied up the unstable ladder of pop stardom with a single-mindedness that is probably inbred in anyone who has already chosen a career by the age of four. She was in a backing band with her brother, Temba, before she was six and by the time producer Koloi Lebona asked her mother's permission to bring her from Cape Town to Johannesburg in 1979, Fassie was a little-known but excellently schooled professional. But Fassie really began to emerge from the wings in 1983 when Brenda and the Big Dudes produced a record called *Weekend Special* which sold 200 000 copies and catapulted the tough-talking performer on to centre stage.

Today, practically every move Brenda Fassie makes is lavishly recorded by the national media. Her wedding last year to Nhlanhla Mbambo was filmed for M-Net. Fassie even composed a song about it on the *Too Late for Mama* album called *Don't Follow Me, I'm Married*. A few weeks ago, it was Fassie's husband who followed her to a Swaziland hotel where, in the middle of the casino, he knocked out her teeth with a punch that accused her of having let another man do exactly that. Of course, the incident made front page headlines.

"I don't know why I got married," she sighs, running her tongue over the temporary, uncomfortable bridge in her mouth. "I do want to have babies ... but I don't know if I want to have his anymore, although I still have this soft spot for him ..."

There is not the slightest tinge of bruised defeat in Fassie's voice when she speaks about her turbulent marriage or, for that matter, anything else. She is the self-styled queen of South African pop, and queens don't hold on to their thrones by crumpling up like used tissues in public. Fassie grew up in an atmosphere of basic survival and, anyway, she's had to resort to physical forms of persuasion once or twice herself.

"I'm strong," she says. "Where I come from, arguments that couldn't be sorted out reasonably would have to be sorted out in other ways ... it usually works when all else fails.

"I've been called a bully, cheeky, forceful, even ill-mannered – and maybe that's how I look from afar, but I think I'm a pretty nice person and at least nobody does my talking for me. I don't hide behind anyone.

"When Miriam Makeba was being pressurised to sing at that party organised in her honour, she told her fans: 'If you want me to sing, don't tell me what to sing.' That was great, but if I'd said that, people would have said I was being a bitch ...

"I may not have a beautiful face, but when I'm in a place, even the walls can feel me inside them. I have character. I have confidence, and I don't like being criticised by people who don't understand the person in Brenda."

Artists in the SABC's make-up department pale at the sight of Fassie walking through the door because she refuses to let them anywhere near her. "I know my own face better than anyone else. If someone there insists on making me up, I act as if I've given in. Then, after they have finished painting me, I wash it all off in front of them."

She laughs and asks if I know where she can find a pair of hazel-coloured contact lenses. She already has blue ones and green ones and the longest, curliest pair of false eyelashes ever worn since Twiggy's came unglued.

Fassie is a self-made stylist: she decides what she wears on stage, she works out all her dance routines in front of an enormous mirror in her bedroom, she also manages herself through the Fassie/Mbambo Connection company – or, as it has become known since the tiff with her husband, the Fassie Connection. But now she wants out. "I'm going to close down the company – being my own manager is becoming a headache, I'm becoming too much of a businesswoman. I need more time to concentrate on my music."

A constant stream of people flows into Fassie's office to elicit her permission for this or her opinion of that. Finally, she snaps, "Let's get out of here," and the interview is resettled in her favourite restaurant at the Johannesburg Sun.

From the moment Fassie sweeps up to the entrance of the hotel, blasting pedestrians out of her path with the car's hooter and shrieking with laughter as a clump of strolling soldiers scatters in fright, she turns on the celebrated charm tap and is given the full treatment. The doorman leaps forward to help her out of the car, then jogs back to the entrance to usher her in. By this time, a small knot of people has stopped and stared and recognised her and there is a brief moment of excitement before Fassie disappears inside.

Suddenly Fassie spots the reigning Miss South Africa, Suzette van der Merwe, eating lunch with a group of business executives at the next table. She also spies a camera.

"Hi, Suzette, my name's Brenda and I just want to say how much I love you and I think the speech you made when you won Miss South Africa was great. Let's have our picture taken together!"

A portable telephone arrives along with her avocado salad and, in between phone calls, she talks about the pitfalls of "politics". On this subject, as on most others, Fassie is unusually honest: "I didn't know what sanctions were until Mandela was released – it was the first time I became aware of them, probably because I read everything he had to say.

"But I want to know why the people who accuse me of cashing in on the political situation by writing songs with a political content are always the first ones to ask me to do a charity performance for nothing. I don't accuse them of cashing in on me.

"I go with the fashion, with what people want to hear."

Fassie's newest album is called *Black President* and yes, the title track is about Nelson Mandela. But it is not on the strength of this record that she has been invited to perform at the ANC-linked Zabalaza Festival in London next month. She has been invited to Zabalaza because it would be ludicrous, at a festival dedicated to current South African culture, to ignore the most popular black female vocalist in the country, even if, in her own words, she's not "politically clued-up".

June 26 1990

Gus goes to hell. Odd, it feels like home
Gus Silber

It's only a game. It's only a game. It's only a game. Mumbling the mantra to myself, I rise from my chair at some ungodly hour of the morning, my head swimming with visions of fire and blood and hulking beasts from the jaws of hell. Not that it's a problem. I'm an adult, right?

I can tell the difference between "virtual" and "reality", between a simulated electronic environment and the real world around my computer terminal. I know for a fact that I am not really an interplanetary stormtrooper, fighting a lone battle to the death against legions of monsters and zombies in a festering toxic netherworld.

I'm fine, really. I know where to draw the line. All I have to do is walk away from my computer, get some sleep, and ... quick! Something in the shadows. I spin around, reach for my plasma rifle, pump screeching blue bolts of electricity across the room. Oh. It's the cat. Look, let's be honest about this. It is *not* only a game. It is Doom.

If you haven't heard of it, if you haven't played it, you've probably been living in some weird, far-flung corner of the universe for the past couple of years. Well, so have I. The difference is, I've been playing Doom. Using nothing but my wits, reflexes and a plasma rifle, rocket launcher, shotgun, chaingun, pistol, chainsaw, fist and BFG9000 laser-blaster, I have been to hell on Mars (Doom I) and hell on Earth (Doom II), and let me tell you, it's beginning to feel just like home.

Soon to be a major motion picture starring Arnold Schwarzenegger, Doom is the first computer game to cross the threshold between mere suspension of disbelief and actual physical discomfort. Play it for a few hours at a stretch, eyes glued to the screen, fingers riveted to keyboard, mouse or joystick, and you soon begin to feel the delirious, draining effects of DIMSS – Doom-induced motion sickness syndrome. Your eyes water, your head hurts, you feel dizzy, short of breath and queasy all over. So who's complaining?

It's a small price to pay for Doom's smoothly gliding cinematic interface, which puts you dead bang in the middle of the hell-raising action. Light sources and textures change convincingly as you cruise the labyrinth, and the recoil from a double-barrelled shotgun blast is almost enough to knock you out of your chair. But that's just atmospherics.

The real guts of Doom lies in its lovingly rendered ultraviolence, topped by a range of real-death sound effects that will chill you to the bone.

Blast a combat-suited Former Human with your shotgun and watch him fall with a gush of blood and the bellow of a wounded bovine. Fire your BFG9000 at a pack of advancing monsters, and watch them vaporise with a sound that is midway between frying bacon and a short-circuiting fuse. Plunge your chainsaw into a grunting, growling, fire-spewing beast from hell, and ... you get the picture.

This is not the kind of program you would want impressionable children or Bishop Peter Storey to see. Then again, at least there is nothing gratuitous about Doom's ballistic orgy of destruction.

You are the good guy, and your mission is to annihilate armies of terrible mutants who seem to have escaped straight from the pages of Revelations. There are the Demons, gorilla-like hulks with freshly peeled flesh and razor-sharp fangs. There are the Lost Souls, screaming green skulls that fly straight towards your face. There are the Cacodemons, gigantic one-eyed heads that belch ball lightning.

There are a whole bunch of others on a whole bunch of levels, and you can pit yourself against them by collecting your weapons one at a time, working out where the secret passages are and using your finer motor skills and instincts to sidestep oblivion and make it to the next level. Or you can cheat.

If, like me, you are the sort of person who seeks instant catharsis rather than intellectual stimulation from a computer game, a few simple codes will give you all the weapons and ammo your heart desires. You can also make yourself invisible, or even invincible, by stepping into the modestly named God Mode of play. But where's the fun in that?

The premise of Doom is that you are a human battling non-humans, and it only makes any sense if you too are susceptible to sudden and violent annihilation. But the really fun thing about Doom is its almost infinite range of possibilities. Sick of Former Humans? Bored stiff with Cacodemons? Simply log on to your neighbourhood bulletin board to the Internet, and take your pick from hundreds of free add-ins that transform Doom's vile monsters into anything from Bill Clinton to Bart Simpson to Barney the purple dinosaur.

My personal favourite replaces Doom's pounding rock soundtrack with the sweet strains of Vivaldi's *Four Seasons*, and the brutish zombie marines with generic yuppie stockbrokers in collar and tie. Handy for those days when your unit trust prices experience a slight "correction" on the Johannesburg Stock Exchange.

Just one word of warning, fellow Doomers. No matter how much you relish this gloriously anti-social game, no matter how much valuable television-watching time you may waste on its various levels of bedlam, try to remember this one thing. It's only a game. It's only a game. It's only a game. It's ...

PC Review, February 1995

Kak or culture?
Kit Peel

"I heard about it at the hairdressers," the lady in the next seat explained. "When the ballet came to Springs last year, my hairdresser told me that it was disgusting. A load of queers leaping about the place," she said.

I was at a performance by the Russian National Ballet in Springs on October 26. My neighbour, who had sneaked into the front row during the interval, was giving me the low-down. "Ag, there are so many ignorant people in Springs, they'd rather spend R99 on a Michael Jackson concert than come to this wonderful spectacle."

With ticket sales of 300 (100 more than last year's performance), the civic hall was still only half full. Lots of mothers and dressy teenage daughters, oldsters, and the occasional stray male. The other men, I discovered earlier, were also watching men in tights. American wrestling on TV in a nearby bar.

Instead of Little Red Riding Hood and the wolf dancing to a Tchaikovsky score, there was "The Rock" throwing the "British Bulldog" into a metal chair.

It was extraordinary. Here was a highly respected Russian ballet company, which has danced in Europe, the United States and the Far East, in a lesser-known backwater of Gauteng. Worse still, the ballet's itinerary in South Africa also included Potchefstroom, Welkom and Pietermaritzburg. I had heard from friends who saw a performance in Pretoria on October 24 that they danced to music played from giant speakers, instead of an orchestra. That night one speaker was off until after interval. "Gosh," my friend commented, "those poor Russians must really be desperate." Two days later, tongue-in-cheek article in mind, I headed out to Springs to see what was going on.

I was to meet with artistic director Serguei Radtchenko and impresario Edouard Miasnikov at the civic hall before the ballet's afternoon rehearsal. Falling foul to the local pastime of misdirecting outsiders, I arrived late, by which time the dancers were already limbering up.

Radtchenko, artistic director and founder of the Russian National Ballet, quickly shattered my illusion of skid-row Russians. "We like coming to South Africa," he said, "it is a change from the usual tours, to Europe or America. It is also a lot warmer than Russia at this time of year! OK, some of the venues are not so great, but we are professionals, we must work in any circumstances." The speakers, he explained, were preferable to using orchestras that are often cobbled together at the last minute.

The Russian National Ballet was founded in 1989. Radtchenko's aim was to bring together the highest classical elements of the Bolshoi and Maryinsky Ballet companies into an independent new company. In its 10 years, the company has toured worldwide to great acclaim and subsequent re-engagements.

Among the ballet community in South Africa there is mixed reaction towards these journeyman companies. "It's often seen as just another group

Derek Bauer

of Russian dancers coming to try and make it in South Africa to get money," explains Johannesburg ballet teacher Alex Lemaitre.

The Cape Town Orchestra's struggle for survival last week highlighted an even greater problem: the South African "culture clash". In response to the orchestra's plea for a R3-million lifeline, local government first queried the orchestra's representativeness and its relevance in a city in which many inhabitants live in abject poverty. As impresario (that is, organiser/promoter) Miasnikov knows, the arts in South Africa have become politicised.

Miasnikov is in a doubly difficult situation. On the one hand, ballet is seen as elitist and not part of popular South African culture. Also, what sponsorship there is for ballet in this country is reserved for home-grown companies, not visiting ones. This is short-sighted, he says.

"If strong artists come to South Africa from Russia, England or America it can only help South African culture. People here can see the top professional standards. It will help them. There was a far higher standard of performance this year by the Russian National Ballet, even though they were using the same dancers. Why? Because since last year they have performed overseas, they have worked with the top international companies and learned from them."

Miasnikov, from 1972 to 1991 the principal clarinettist at the Bolshoi Theatre's symphony orchestra, and now with our own National Symphony Orchestra, is trying to bring ballet to a wider audience. For this reason the Russian National Ballet can be seen not just in Pretoria, Johannesburg, Durban or Cape Town but in such culturally suburban places as Springs. Ballet can catch on in this country, Miasnikov believes. In the programme he is quoted as saying: "Ballet is a form of art which is loved and understood all over the world, with no regional frontiers or barriers." On the evening of October 26 I was in the right place to put this theory to the test.

Sitting behind me in the second row, my cultural guinea pig waited. A scowling teenage girl was muttering what sounded like "kak" to her friend. Culture versus kak, it was a national dilemma.

The first half began with three short pieces. An uneventful Tchaikovsky number, a stunning Spanish dance (as much flamenco as ballet) and Rachmaninov's *Spring Waters*. Behind me the chatter resolutely continued. The Paquita ballet, the tale of a Spanish gypsy girl in love with a Napoleonic officer, saw the tide begin to turn. Flashy dancing, gorgeous costumes and an old-fashioned love story proved a real crowd-pleaser. Every other leap was met with applause.

In the interval I discovered a group of women artists from Ghana. They were exhibiting their work in Benoni that weekend. In the meantime, their hosts had arranged the trip to Springs. It was their first glimpse of ballet and they were enthusiastic about it. Was it relevant to Africa, I asked. "Of course," they laughed, "everyone can see that it is beautiful."

The second half was taken up solely by act three of Tchaikovsky's *Sleeping Beauty*. A medley of fairy tales starring Little Red Riding Hood and the wolf, Goldilocks and a bear, the bluebird and his princess among others. It was the high point of the evening. Little Red Riding Hood pursued by the wolf, the bluebird and princess soaring across the stage. My seat-hopping neighbour was enthralled. Looking back I saw that the scowl had gone. Culture had won, the girl was enjoying herself. The Russian dancers closed to rapturous applause and Miasnikov had been proved right.

Much of the criticisms laid against ballet were, as the evening showed, clearly untrue. It may carry an elitist badge, but it sure had popular appeal. The combination of music and dance told a story in a way that everyone could follow. The dazzle of the staging and costumes and the constant movement of the dance also ensure against the darker side of classical music, boredom.

"We must get people interested in this. We can make this one culture for everybody," Miasnikov says. He has a point. After all, if it can work in Springs, why not in the rest of South Africa?

November 12 1999

It's wonderful weed!

Rant Boy

Rant Boy was a bit frightened by a headline last week, in the local rag Barry Ronge so butchly calls *L'Etoile*. The headline read "Dagga – a proven heart risk" – and anyone who knows Rant Boy would realise how frightening that could be. (And if you don't know Rant Boy, hit the archives - you'll get the picture.)

But then Rant Boy took a closer look at the report, and saw the huge, representative sample of heart-attack patients who'd been studied – less than 4 000 (that's not even a week's coronary deaths in the US). And, boys and girls, of the 4 000 people studied, less than 4% had, at some point in their lives, smoked dagga. Let me put that another way – more than 96% of heart-attack patients have never touched the weed in their lives, and Johannesburg's biggest daily paper is touting it as a heart risk. (I can't wait for next week's headline: "Red meat – deadlier than dope!")

So, in the face of this kind of disinformation, Rant Boy presents a little poem for you. (Actually, you could probably sing this poem to the tune of *Under the Sea*, from *The Little Mermaid*, but then the Disney Corporation would probably sue you. So don't.) The verse was originally inspired by then-president Nelson Mandela's remark that South Africans who emigrate are unpatriotic, a statement which Rant Boy found a tad simplistic – hence he came up with a fabulous reason to stay. Here goes …

They say grass is always greener, that grows in your neighbour's turf;
And that is why frightened white folk be trying to fly to Perth.
Though they might feel safe and wealthy in their new adopted clime,
There is one local tradition they're gonna have to leave behind …
Wonderful weed! Wonderful weed!

From Brazil to Benghazi, they speak of our Swazi with wonder indeed!

'Cos if you buy from an Aussie bloke, one small bankie costs as much as coke –

They don't sell to the nation, from their petrol stations, this wonderful weed!

It's the same in the other countries to which our new exiles fly.

Though they live in a First World homeland, I bet they miss the old Transkei.

Got a laptop, got a cellphone – they got a new Mercedes-Benz.

But they'd trade it all in, I know for ... a chillum with their Durban friends!

Wonderful weed! Wonderful weed!

When friends come a-calling, we start a-mauling, just take out the seeds!

And then we grow them when times get hard, with our green fingers in our own backyard –

I'm not emigrating, I can't be forsaking, this wonderful weed!

So I appeal to ex-president Madiba, and present President Mbeki:

Prove yourselves true renaissance leaders; set the African sacrament free.

Build our houses; feed our livestock; make some paper, save some trees;

Make some petrol; make some fabric; ease the sufferings of HIV.

Wonderful weed! Wonderful weed!

Let rural abantu grow just what they want to; with weed they'll succeed!

And if those Yankee pirates wail, we'll simply tell them they don't have to inhale ...

I'm staying, patriotic; stop being idiotic – it's wonderful weed!

ZA@PLAY, March 28 2000

Part Six
Change is Pain

A sinister horde of puffing peaceniks
Anton Harber

The problem was this: How do you motivate a bunch of unfit intellectuals, paunchy pacifists and flat-footed feminists to jog 5km around Zoo Lake? The solution was simple: bring the South African Police, preferably the riot squad.

That was the case at the Run for Peace at Zoo Lake last Sunday, when the boys in blue provided a breakthrough in sporting medicine that should be noted by anyone trying to organise a fun run for those who find no fun in running.

Before the riot squad arrived at the Run for Peace this week, it promised to be no more than a slightly unusual Sunday jog around the lake.

If it was unusual, it was only because most of those dressed in takkies, shorts and "Stop Apartheid" T-shirts appeared to be better equipped for drawing up petitions, putting up posters and discoursing on the finer points of the Freedom Charter than for voluntary physical exertion on a fine summer afternoon.

These were people who thought going for a trot meant launching a polemic against a member of the Fourth International.

But the sight of the riot squad at the starting post had all of them stubbing out their cigarettes, sucking in their stomachs, puffing out their chests and doing warm-up exercises as an act of defiance.

And when lawyer Kathy Satchwell stood up to tell the crowd that the City Council had withdrawn permission for the event, ageing activists who had come as spectators were suddenly shouting, "Let's run."

But the final straw came from the riot squad commander. He took a megaphone and warned the crowd that it constituted an illegal gathering and it had 15 minutes to disperse.

Suddenly, everyone's adrenalin was pumping. There was no further need for warm-up exercises. People who had been dubious about strolling around the 5km course were suddenly running on the spot like veteran marathoners.

Someone stood up and suggested that the crowd obey the police and disperse at a slow jog along the planned route.

The Run for Peace was on. Now it was no normal run; it had become a major news event.

Bruce Fordyce was there to lead the way. The foreign television crews were there to be arrested. Sheena Duncan was there to issue a statement, the Detainees Parents Support Committee was there to analyse the results and issue a monthly report, and Neil McCarthy was there to play the part of a young, muscular hunk for whom 5km was something one did before breakfast.

A Peace Run, of course, has its own rules. No overtaking on the right, for example. The route has to have no sharp turns to the left – it must be a good, straight path forward. No separate route for women.

It was a fairly easy, flat route. A young bunch of Black Sash members took an early lead in the car park, but were soon overtaken by the Yeoville activists, whose training had come from being on the run since the Emergency began.

The Yeovillites, however, got caught in a difficult polemic along Lower Park Drive, allowing the liberals into the vanguard.

But the liberals stopped for a smoke along Jan Smuts Avenue, there was a resurgence of radicalism, and the Yeovillites regained the lead along the final straight.

The Brixton workerists did not fare at all, since most of them were off launching some joggers' federation in Durban.

The run quickly developed its own style. There was someone doing what he called "the Sebe step" (running backwards); there was the "Mangope meander" (hopping on one leg); there was the Jodac jaunt (two steps forward, one step backward) and the "Convention Movement special" (the three-legged race).

And, of course, there were the ultra-left deviationists who cut across the bowling green and knocked 500m off the course.

In the end, the police did no more than take down a few names (mostly of foreign television crews) and photograph everyone.

I expect to appear on *Police File* any day now: "Unfit jogger wanted for causing unrest in Zoo Lake area. Last seen in first aid tent."

But the police can rest assured. As well-known activists collapsed on the roadside clutching their sides, gasping for air, I knew why apartheid still existed: concerned citizens are not yet fit to run the country.

But the authorities should not rest too easy. At the end of the run, one of the fitter concerned citizens still had enough strength to drag himself to his feet and suggest that this become a regular Sunday afternoon event.

So, providing the police play their part and come along to provide the adrenalin, you can expect a Run for Peace at 5pm every Sunday afternoon at Zoo Lake.

Results will be announced in the SAP's Monday morning unrest report.

December 6 1985

Derek Bauer

Do you plead unguilty or not unguilty?

Ivor Powell

The gallery curator tried to pursue the point: "Let's say, just hypothetically, that the Appeal Board reverses the decision and finds that the work is, in fact, desirable ..."

"Not undesirable," said the nameless one.

"I beg your pardon."

"The opposite of 'undesirable' is not 'desirable' but 'not undesirable'." The lips, as I imagine them, pursed.

This conversation took place some time last week (although I've obviously invented some details) in the plush and air-conditioned confines of the Shell House in Plein Street. The subject was a rather unusual piece of sculpture made by Michelle Raubenheimer, a postgraduate student at Wits. It was being exhibited along with work by other postgraduate students from the Wits fine arts department at Shell South Africa's plush ground-level showpiece gallery.

Poor Shell! This turned out to be a very dubious kind of promotion of the Shell corporate identity. The shadow people moved in, the (bless them) guardians of our public morality. And the work was prodded and interrogated and pinched and scrutinised through various coloured filters. And the lips pursed and the stamp came out; and the stamp fell. And the stamp read UNDESIRABLE.

So Michelle Raubenheimer's sculpture was banned. The four artists exhibiting with her, in consultation with their promoter, Professor Alan Crump, head of the fine arts department at Wits, did the only thing they could do. They withdrew their work in sympathy, or perhaps in anger. Shell SA did nothing. The exhibition was duly closed. And that was that.

What I want to know, though, is: if a work is to be judged either undesirable or not undesirable, how shall a person be presumed until found not unguilty?

This is not, in this particular instance, a fatuous question. In one sense, of course, the censors' semantic point, however *1984*-ishly formulated, is valid enough. The fact that the state should find a particular work not absolutely undesirable does not mean that it positively endorses it.

But let's look at the scenario. Your work is deemed undesirable. OK. You have two options.

Either you remove the work from exhibition and you appeal. Or you remove the work from exhibition and you don't appeal.

If you appeal and your appeal is upheld, then you may go ahead and reinstate the now no longer undesirable work on your exhibition.

Thanks a lot. By this stage your exhibition will in all likelihood – given the average three-week run of art exhibitions in this country – have been over for some months. So either way you lose; your two options come down to the proverbial dog's chance and no chance at all.

In effect, what the intervention of the censors means in the case of an art exhibition (and equally in the case of a theatrical production) is that you are tried and condemned by the investigating officer. Whether you are found unguilty or not unguilty in the trial is utterly irrelevent.

That's a big responsibility for a single person to carry on merely human shoulders. Fortunately, though, the secret agent of the national psyche has, to assist him or her in the discharge of these solemn duties, a publication called *Guidelines with Regard to Section 47 (2) Act 42 of 1974* (sic – that should read 1984). It just so happens that I also have in my possession a copy of this particular document.

And what a storehouse of almost scholastic subtlety it is, too. It grapples with and finally subdues such demons of the midnight imagination as: "How many nipple stars between the covers of a single publication should be taken to constitute an arousal to lustfulness?" (The answer parenthetically is: Somewhat fewer than the number of angels that can dance on the head of a pin.)

It sets up such infallible tests of undesirability as the following: "If recourse is constantly had to concepts like 'blatantly shameless' and 'repulsive', scenes of this kind should in any case be judged on their own merits."

It draws an edge as clean as a razor blade between profanities like "Goddammit", "Oh my God" and "God", which are not considered undesirable "unless their use is blatant" – I'm still struggling with that one, but I'll let you know when I work it out – and those of the type "Jesus", "Christ" and "Jesus Christ", which will have syllables excised "so that the continuity of the dialogue can be preserved".

But then I'm getting off the point. The relevant criteria are as follows: "Determine whether the relevant moral principle is impaired in an indecent manner by the material, in other words in a blatantly shameless or sickly manner or in a manner intended to arouse lustfulness ... Mere infringement of the relevant moral principle is not enough ... Only repugnant or repulsive infringement is undesirable."

So now you know. How does it feel, Ms Raubenheimer, to have thrown the so-called reasonable man into such a state of agitation? Good, I hope. Because, as I see it, the nameless censor was absolutely right in one sense – about the work. It is obscene. It does impair the relevant moral principle.

But at the same time it's a very good piece of sculpture. The two - and this is really the problem with censorship in this particular case, if not in general – are by no means incompatible.

This is especially true in a case where the "relevant moral principle" is precisely what the work is directed against. The point is that Michelle Raubenheimer's figure, with its phallic torso and its oily face distorted by mindless lust and staring at its own inflamed vagina, presents a critical vision of those sexual values that dominate the society we live in – those values that characterise the "reasonable man", those values that shine through the text from which I have been quoting.

It presents through satire an image of that prurience which sexual repression both breeds and sustains. It is obscene, but that is only because it attempts to confront the spectator with an obscenity. By doing this it serves a moral function; it promotes an evolution of moral standards and attitudes.

By the same token, a society that cannot accommodate criticism of this kind condemns itself to moral stagnation.

But then maybe that's the point.

November 8 1985

Zapiro

Blue land of puffballs join hands, ooh yeah

Gus Silber

South Africans of all colours, creeds, political persuasions, puffball skirts, padded jackets and hairdos came together in virtual harmony for the Third National Song Festival on TV1 on Saturday night. For almost 20 minutes, aesthetically sensitive gremlins delayed the live crossing to the Standard Bank Arena, forcing the SABC to fill the gap with a random recital by Bles Bridges.

Gremlins did not delay the crossing to Bles Bridges, however, leaving him with no option but to exorcise the gremlins that were keeping him glued to the screen. As it turned out, Bles was one of the few South African singers, indeed, one of the few South Africans, who had not come to the Standard Bank Arena to sing a song about Africa, land of sunshine, Lord, why can't we live together, ooh yeah.

Part of the answer lay in the fact that South Africa was divided by law into 17 ethnic regional radio stations, each of whom had sent along a person or persons to sing a song about national togetherness. This went on for three hours, excluding gremlins, by which time the nation was united in its passionate conviction that national song festivals organised by regional radio stations should be heard and not seen on national television stations.

Nevertheless, there were highlights. The festival was opened by a group called Slam singing a song called *Life*, which failed as a song but succeeded as a moving and powerful argument for euthanasia. "We are here today, where are we tomorrow, nobody knows, nobody cares," mimed a blonde in an electric-blue dress and electrified perm, while two embarrassed blokes mimed individually co-ordinated dance steps behind her.

Thus was the artistic yardstick and appropriate audience response established for yet another SABC in-house outside broadcast extravaganza, in which the spotlights were blue and purple and the set was like the inside of a prism and the separate but equal co-presenters looked like wine stewards and the silhouette of the floor manager could be seen gesticulating frantically in the foreground.

"And that was Benjamin Dube with his rendition of *Save the World* for Radio Metro," blinked co-presenter Coenie de Villiers, while co-presenter Treasure Tshabalala consulted his cue cards and announced that Debbie Young was going to sing *Where Do We Go from Here, Africa?*.

The answer was as far away as possible. "We really love ya, Africa, people are dying and others are flying all over the world." In a country that already has two national anthems, the desirability of an annual multi-ethnic national song festival needs to be justified at the highest official level. The only rational explanation must be that the festival provides a much-needed platform for struggling designers of chintz puffball skirts and electric-blue frocks made from discarded discotheque reflector balls.

So many female singers wore electric-blue frocks, and so many female backing singers, ranged in descending order from fattest to least fattest, wore chintz puffball skirts, that it was a relief to see Gene and Duane Rockwell wearing matt-black dinner suits with matching rugby balls under the shoulders. The relief, however, was only relative.

"Growing up ain't easy," they groaned in unison, while throwing up was. Then Karleen Loader, introduced as a veteran of 20 years in showbiz who had toured with Rolf Harris, sang *Through the Eyes of a Child*, a tribute to her remarkable memory as well as her platinum blonde hairdo. But what about Africa?

"Land of sunshine, land of promise, we're gonna join together, Africa our strength is unity," serenaded Carla Carson, wearing an electric-red bikini top and beaded headband in solidarity with the rest of Africa. Clearly, we were running out of electric-blue frocks as well as time.

Treasure Tshabalala introduced William Mathethwa: "One of the first few people to form a trust fund for the well-known Mathibela twins."

As if this wasn't enough, he then became one of the first few people to sing a song about the well-known Natal floods, entitled *Floods*.

At last, the evening's highlight. The end. In a dazzling sequence specially choreographed for radio listeners, a large purple blackboard flashed scores from 17 regional radio stations while the co-presenters painstakingly repeated the scores for people listening on stereo radio.

Next time, I think I'll tune in.

August 26 1988

No easy wait for the legend's freedom

Charlotte Bauer

Is it just possible that the exiles didn't come home last week because they wanted to watch Nelson Mandela's release on a decent television channel?

Between SABC TV's 3pm link-up with its crew outside the Victor Verster prison in Paarl and the Magic Moment an hour and 10 minutes later, we were subjected to:

- Clarence Keyter doing a bad imitation of William Wordsworth: "The sun is baking down on us ... the sun, not only needed for growing grapes, but for a growing South Africa"... "Here we stand outside the most beautiful prison in the world" ... "The people are getting a bit impatient – but they are waiting patiently"... (Take your pick);
- Guitar renditions of the *Turkish Rondo* while we waited, music which contributed to the atmosphere of the occasion only inasmuch as the furious thumpings of parish piano players once enhanced the drama of silent movies ... do do doodeloo doodeloo de loo ...;

- Tedious shots of the wall outside Victor Verster which, if we stared at it long enough and thought beautiful thoughts, would surely collapse, à la Berlin, all by itself.

The stepmother of the nation, of course, arrived at the last possible moment – almost on the dot of 3pm. One couldn't help wondering whether she had ever managed to collect her children from school on time. This muse led to further wondering about whether her husband was wondering the same thing – after all, she did have 27 years in which to rehearse this particular appointment.

Naturally, all this wondering served little purpose, but it beat the hell out of swaying in time to the *Turkish Rondo* while Clarence searched his brain for interesting things to say ("Oh look, here comes a man singing and dancing - such people are known throughout Africa as praise singers").

But Clarence was right about one thing: the tension, as they say, was mounting. About 4pm I glanced through a window on to what is normally one of the busiest roads in Johannesburg, even on a Sunday afternoon. The street was quite empty and a gouty tortoise could have crossed the road in safety.

An estimated one billion people around the globe were glued to their television sets. I have no idea what the people who don't have television sets were doing, but I can vouch for the fact they weren't walking down Market Street.

And then the diaphanous veils of 27-years' worth of mystery were lifted and Nelson Mandela came walking down the middle of the road leading away from the prison.

The walk to freedom, as he himself once predicted in a book title, was not easy. Suddenly, he turned at the gate and started walking back up the road ... what's this? He can't handle it. The sight of 3 000 grunting zoom lenses has proved too much for the man. His courage has failed him.

He's going back inside ...

But he was merely seeking refuge in the car that would drive him to Cape Town, very sensibly avoiding the possibility of being lovingly trampled to death by adoring fans.

As the black, green and gold of the African National Congress flag moved slowly across our picture, Mandela moved slowly down the street, his expression inscrutably sage-like, his hand in Winnie's.

After 27 years, it was his privilege not to look hot and bothered, unlike Cyril Ramaphosa, who walked backwards before the living legend, swatting people out of the way and sweating profusely.

Twenty-four hours or so earlier, at his smoothly handled press conference, FW de Klerk's only gaffe was grammatical.

It was also appropriate.

"We must uplift the State of Emergency," the president said.

On Sunday afternoon, the dignified appearance of Nelson Mandela went some way to uplifting the sorry, sorry state South Africa finds itself in.

February 12 1990

Gatecrashing the National Party

Arthur Maimane

My search for an entry point into the ruling class had an inauspicious start across the street from the Johannesburg Art Gallery in Joubert Park. I asked people on the pavement which was King George Street and none were quite certain: "It's somewhere around here," was the best advice.

In fact we were at an intersection of the street on which the National Party constituency offices for Jeppe are located. The entrance into

Lourenco Court is dark and I had to fumble my way to the NP door on which a notice said "please ring the bell". Except that in the darkness I couldn't find the bell.

I barged into the well-lit but empty offices and only after knocking on a burglar-proofed frosted glass door – "Who's knocking on that door!" a woman's voice demanded – did I finally find two secretaries who were surprised that I'd got through the party's security screen into the front office.

But they were polite and not particularly surprised when I explained I wanted to be the first black member of the ruling party – if the NP congress in Durban later this month decides to go non-racial in the new South Africa.

I was advised to speak to the constituency member of Parliament – who was in Pretoria for the day but would be available on Friday – about my intentions.

I had better luck at the constituency offices for Auckland Park, which are in a former private house. The front door was opened by Richard McArthur, a well-spoken and courteous young man who turned out to be just the person I was looking for. He invited me into the boardroom for a chat. He too was not surprised by my intention to be black NP Member 001.

But, he told me, I couldn't join until the decision was made in Durban: "And I hope it'll be the right decision, because we need all the allies we can get."

Once this "right" decision had been taken by a previously right-wing party, joining would be a mere formality. I could sign up on Day One of the new, open era and there wouldn't even be a membership fee to pay: "If you ask people to pay, they're likely to say they'll do it next year."

All that was asked by the NP, McArthur told me, was a donation to party funds: "Usually about R2 for which you get the *Nationalist* free every month."

Like the women opposite Joubert Park, McArthur was not surprised by my interest in joining his party and assured me there would be no objections in Auckland Park. Perhaps, I suppose, because they have elected Roelf Meyer, who is a well-known verligte.

Despite suspicions and allegations that the state was orchestrating the current violence in the townships, McArthur expressed concern about this week's slaughter on the East Rand.

Did I think it would continue? he asked. I fervently replied that I hoped it would not. What did I think was the cause? I disclaimed any political expertise without telling him that as a "returnee" I didn't know enough of the background and only had theories.

When we parted McArthur gave me a copy of the party paper and other glossy documents detailing NP policy.

August 17 1990

Madam & Eve

The Foot-in-Mouth Awards

Krisjan Lemmer

You know, it really has been a vintage year for *skinderpraatjies*. And since this is the season for giving and not getting, Oom Krisjan has decided not to ask for any more *skandaal*, but to reward the best of your work. Wonderfully well done!

So on behalf of myself and the entire panel at the Dorsbult Bar – and of course Klipdrift, our unofficial sponsors – I give you the 1990 Golden Lemmers.

Here we go.

The Open Wide to Change Feet Award

Bronze to the union official who assured patients at strike-hit hospitals they would be cared for by "skeleton structures".

Silver to *The Star,* who reported that a Germiston traffic officer had been wounded in the leg "after it went through the chest of a suspected burglar, killing the man".

And the golden Lemmer, to the newsreader for this report on fighting in Natal: "Reports say the police encouraged [pause] ... I'm sorry, that should be encountered fighting factions."

The McEnroe Memorial "You Cannot Be Serious" Award

The bronze in this category goes to the Transkei police spokesman who announced a clampdown on toyi-toying on Wild Coast beaches: "This sometimes scares the tourists. It must be borne in mind that nations other than Africans are not gifted to sing and dance effectively at the same time. They sometimes regard this simultaneous action as violent."

The silver goes to playwright Deon Opperman for this press release: "For director Deon Opperman, the play was a challenge in more ways than one.

On a technical level he has already decided that Oubaas, the dog, would not be present physically, also not the sheep which is slaughtered on stage every night."

And the golden Lemmer goes to Anglo's former chairman, Gavin Relly, who said his corporation was against monopolies. "In Anglo American we have no experience of them," he said.

The Leon Mellett Medal for New-Style Government

The bronze to Dr John Moodie, director of medical services in the Cape, who said a black patient was not turned away from a Gardens hospital "because of the colour of her skin but because three beds reserved for blacks at the hospital were full".

The silver to the National Productivity Institute, whose report on private clinics came out quickly enough – not so its study of provincial hospitals, which after some time we still await.

And the golden Lemmer goes to the two traffic cops in the Free State, who caught a man in a speed trap – and offered him a R10 raffle ticket in aid of their social club in lieu of a fine.

The Why-Pik-on-Us Prize

The bronze goes to Pik Botha who said: "He is struggling with things like the concept of a multiparty system. They have no experience in this ..." Not talking about FW, but Gorbachev.

The silver goes to unionists and lawyers who hired a room at the Johannesburg Sun to plan their next moves in the OK strike – then had to vacate when the Sun workers also went on strike.

And the golden Lemmer goes to some bewildered *bandiete* up in the north. A South African Defence Force officer, when asked by anxious visitors to a conference in Venda if the temporary strip they were about to land on had been tested, said: "Oh yes. We made a couple of test runs, using about 20 prisoners from the local jail."

The Polson Pen Prize

Bronze goes to the Zambian couple whose birthday greeting to their daughter in a Lusaka newspaper read thus: "Catherine. Please reduce your weight. Mum and dad."

The silver to Nelson Mandela, whose aside to Cyril Ramaphosa went: "You know what job you should have in the new South Africa? General secretary of the National Union of Mineworkers."

And the golden Lemmer goes to *The Citizen* who ran this headline: "Darkies in the pound seats".

The Profound Wisdom of the Common Man Cup

The bronze to the East Rand prostitute who dealt with a man and his wife, who were threatening to set the police on her, by saying: "Don't I know you from somewhere?"

The silver goes to the man in a snobbish shebeen, where everybody had to justify their presence by saying what jobs they do. "I'm involved in medicine," he said. "I'm a patient at Bara."

And the golden Lemmer ... to the doctor at Baragwanath who eventually fended off a northern suburbs caller who insisted that her Malawian gardener was an Aids threat, by saying: "Just make sure he wears a condom each time he mows the lawn."

The Why Bother Any More Award

To the South African Defence Force, a bronze, for cancelling all *"Ken Jou Vyand"* classes.

The silver goes to the black woman who, tired of phoning for central Jo'burg flats and being turned down, decided to say she was white. "Sorry, we only take blacks," was the reply.

And the golden Lemmer ... to the people of Munsieville who marched demanding the council's resignation. Puzzled officials pointed out the people had already forced the council out.

The From the Mouth of Babes Bowl

Bronze to the township kid who, when asked if he knew Mandela's first name, said: "Release."

Silver to the English kid who, when asked what was celebrated over Easter, said: "Mandela's birthday."

And to Rozanne Botha, poetess supreme, a golden Lemmer for this financially astute *gediggie* on her wedding invitation: "At the request of friends/ If you'd like to give a gift/ Spare yourself a fuss/ Set aside a penny or two/ Just for the two of us."

Well done, the winners. It's probably wiser to keep your feet on the ground but it's much more fun sticking them in your mouth. Don't stop now.

December 20 1991

Taking on the white man's burden
John Matshikiza

"To the untrained eye," says Achmat, "these dogs might look a bit lacksy-daisy." "A bit what?" I say. "Yes, they might look a bit lacksy-daisy now, in broad daylight, to you, because you don't know them," Achmat says, "but at night their ears go back flat on their heads, and they're off round the place like a couple of panthers on the prowl."

We look at the two timid old Alsatians, sleeping in whatever shade they can find, and it is hard to believe anything about them, except that they look like more trouble than they're worth.

But the snoozing hounds seem to be a minor detail in the greater scheme of things. We have been house-hunting for weeks, and have finally fetched up in a part of the dreaded northern suburbs that looks like it might finally be an answer that everyone is happy with.

OK, it's not the most fashionable part, and friends and acquaintances are handing out dire warnings about crime and hijacking, but where, we ask, is it possible to live in Johannesburg without these evils? The place we've found suits our collective pocket and actually lives up to the hype in the newspaper ad: huge garden, bathrooms, roof, office space – even a swimming pool.

Now we are going through the famous voetstoots process, the bit where you find out what you're really taking on.

As I understand it, the peculiarly South African concept of voetstoots normally applies to fixtures and fittings – peeling walls, missing taps and so on. But in this case, voetstoots embraces moveable objects as well, some of which, like these dogs, also eat, drink and indulge in associated bodily functions.

Achmat and his family are not the owners. They are the present tenants. But they are promoting everything about the place with the glassy-eyed passion of American tele-evangelists. They are in a hurry for us to love this homestead because they are in a hurry to get out of the country, and if we sign a lease with the landlords, they won't be penalised on the contract they will be breaking by leaving early. It all sounds a bit dubious, but in spite of it all, the place still seems to offer more pros than cons.

So we agree to take on the dogs, in the hope that they'll provide some sort of protection. We turn down the unlicensed gun (Achmat's assurance that "you don't need a licence if you only intend to use it privately on your own property" sounds a bit far out). We also turn down the ageing BMW with the balding tyres, as well as a couple of ugly lounge suites and various other bits of furniture.

Rico

We do, however, agree to buy the TV set and the curtains. We also agree to keep on the maid and the gardener. We're going to need all the help we can get, from people who know the territory and are familiar with the dogs.

With that, all parties are satisfied, and we set a date for Achmat and family to move out and for us to move in. Gentlemanly handshakes are shook all round.

I found out later that we shouldn't have signed anything without having a vicious lawyer, armed escorts, a Home Affairs hit squad and the psychiatric unit of the Society for the Prevention of Cruelty to Animals on our side.

Achmat and company took everything that would be useful in their new lives in the Far East with them (including the curtains and other items we had paid for). They left behind two years' worth of household garbage and a string of problems.

The maid and the gardener were top of the list. They'd had a long-standing hatred for each other, which we hadn't been warned about, and now proceeded to do everything they could to bad-mouth one another and get each other sacked.

The maid accused the gardener of being a substance abuser with homicidal tendencies. The gardener accused the maid of being an illegal alien from Malawi. I was beginning to reel under the weight of what had previously been the white man's burden, and discovering that I was not very good at it.

In the midst of this mayhem, the Alsatians, far from being pillars of strength, were proving to be cowering wretches who never moved far from the safety of the kitchen door. When we discovered that the female was pregnant we thought we would at least have some sturdy pups to train up as savage protectors, but even that dream was shattered when she ate the whole litter as soon as they were born.

We braced ourselves and started firing people. We fired the dogs. We fired the maid when it turned out she was an accomplice in the theft of the curtains and went on long periods of unexplained leave besides. We tried to fire the gardener, but we couldn't find him. He was off on a binge. When he came back he was so badly beaten up we hadn't the heart.

So now we sit on our northern 'burbs ranch and wonder what is going to happen next.

March 26 1999

Life's tough in the northern suburbs
John Matshikiza

The phone has been ringing right off the hook since last week's report about our new beginning in the northern suburbs. This would have been gratifying if it wasn't for the fact that most callers have been obsessed, not with what we've managed to do about our safety, but with two burning questions: did we get a new maid (one that wasn't from Malawi) after we fired the old one, and how are we coping with the maintenance of the swimming pool?

These are both sore points. They are an uncomfortable reminder of the "ying/yang", "them/us" territory we used to inhabit, and its lingering shadow.

The best way I can describe that "them/us" universe is to refer back to my first visual impression of the land of my birth after more than 30 years "overseas".

As the massive aircraft began its final descent, the grey light of the alien Highveld dawn fell across the wintry world that was rushing up to meet us. We swept across some nameless white suburb, where every house had a double garage, manicured lawns, and, yes, the obligatory, dazzlingly blue kidney-shaped pool.

Then, as we swept lower, the first images of some equally nameless black township, mile upon mile of almost unrelieved dust, across which the millions of matchbox houses were strewn with genocidal orderliness. Somewhere down there, between these two worlds, were the people I was coming back to live with.

A week in the township, warm as the bosom of my instantly extended family was, proved to me that I would never regain the long-lost skills of that kind of jungle survival. Education had made me stupid.

At the same time, the thought of living in the north, behind those fortified walls, seemed out of the question. Politically speaking, it just didn't seem to be part of the plan.

On the other hand, some of us had been living for many years among the "thems" of Europe (East and West) and America, and should have grown accustomed to this pastiche-Hollywood lifestyle.

Yes, but not quite. Hollywood is a pastiche of all sorts of other things anyway, and the poolside lifestyle of rich white South Africa was merely a pastiche of a pastiche. How do you get your head into that?

Besides, in the outside world we had chosen to huddle together self-consciously as exiles, rather aloof from the societies we found ourselves in. We weren't planning to be around there for too long. We didn't get sucked into bingo and Beethoven because we were going "home", sooner or later. At "home" we wouldn't need to indulge in such shallow cultural activities.

All very well, but now that we were home, what was there to identify with? Well, that first impression, through the window of the plane, just about said it all. There was not to be much choice beyond the pool-world and the other one.

So now we're part of the pool-world. Obligatory accessories in the pool-world include the Maid, the Private Police Force, and the Barracuda.

And, yes, we did get a new maid. In fact we've had two in succession, but that's a long story. The private police force is a necessary evil that we try to see as little as possible. But it is the pool, and the vicious Barracuda that lurks inside it like a serpent of the deep, that eats up most of our physical and intellectual resources.

I can admit now that a pool was not something that I had given much thought to during the first few decades of my life. It was only when a sharp, Sotho-speaking character driving a Mazda MX-6 came to test the water that I started to get a hang of how little I knew about it. He announced that the black, rubbery quality of the water was a little abnormal, and explained that the pool would have to be drained, chemically cleaned, and then refilled.

I had visions of a man in a wetsuit plunging in and pulling out a plug, releasing tons of water into a subterranean sewage system. Then I imagined it being refilled from a hidden, fold-out tap inside the pool. Nothing like that. The process was both simpler and more complicated, involving the manipulation of pumps and hosepipes.

Then came the endless juggling of lethal chemicals to keep the new water clean. The gardener (who had recovered by this time, by the way) had quite an amusing time watching me weep uncontrollably, my shoes ruined by pool acid and my chest thick with chlorine fumes.

But I got my own back when a rat got stuck up the Barracuda. How this happened I cannot tell, but after a week of failing to get it to wriggle, I took the whole apparatus to the pool shop. They looked at me like I was mad, and showed me the head of a rat sticking out of the machinery. Since they wouldn't remove it, I had to delegate the task to George. It was a pretty foul business, but George doesn't snigger at me anymore.

I think this means that I have arrived.

April 2 1999

The beginner's guide to "perfectly legitimate behaviour"

Paul Kirk, Jubie Matlou, Ivor Powell, Mungo Soggot and Evidence wa ka Ngobeni

The public reaction to *Mail & Guardian* revelations that Minister of Home Affairs Mangosuthu Buthelezi is being investigated for the alleged receipt of millions of rands in pay-offs from KwaZulu-Natal's illegal casino operators confirms that South Africa's capacity for tolerating corruption has scaled new heights.

On Friday morning the *M&G*'s phone lines burned with the opprobrium of irate callers. "That poster ...!" they howled. But they were not referring to the poster about Buthelezi's casino millions.

It was the other billboard, the one that said: "F*** You, Hansie Cronje", which inspired such hatred. Not a murmur about an article presenting documentary evidence that a minister of state was salting away in his personal bank account a fortune in illicit payments.

We venture that whole governments would have been brought down in other parts of the world by only half of the amount in question. Fortunately, we have been helped out of our bewilderment. Responding to the most recent set of revelations, Mario Oriani-Ambrosini, Buthelezi's long-serving adviser, said the minister saw no reason to answer these charges.

The *M&G* had already demonstrated its malfeasance, Oriani-Ambrosini thundered, when, in March, we wrote about the supermarket bags full of R50 notes, choosing to portray such "perfectly legitimate behaviour" as somehow improper.

OK, Mr Oriani-Ambrosini, you win.

For argument's sake, let us accept that a Cabinet minister riffling through R2-million ... in R50 notes ... in Checkers packets ... in Ulundi's First

National Bank is "perfectly legitimate behaviour [PLB]". We should perhaps then take the opportunity to compile a guide to other forms of "PLB" that have taken root or have persisted in the new South Africa.

Herewith, then, the *M&G* beginner's guide to a few of the many variations of PLB. We make no claim to comprehensiveness in this hasty compilation, but hope that what follows will at least provide a framework for further explorations.

High-road solutions to traffic snarl-ups

A R50 note discreetly inserted into an identity document and handed over to a traffic officer could rescue an offender from far heavier fines and/or the inconvenience of court appearances. This simple expedient is known to be especially effective in the festive season when traffic officers, like the rest of us, are looking for that extra bit of cheer.

Alternatively, one may choose to cough up half the value of any ticket that actually gets written out, and offer this to a diligent member of the clerical staff of the traffic department, who will duly delete any record of the offence from the system. Like the R50 payout, this method has the advantage of eliminating unwanted middlemen, like the traffic department and the state, from the transaction.

Acquiring a driver's licence can also prove less daunting than it might appear at first, at least to those schooled in the subtle and slippery arts of PLB.

You would seem to need the status of a deputy speaker of Parliament to actually pass a driver's test in absentia, but R400 will secure the legal document as long as you are prepared to go through the motions of being tested. It does not really matter how dramatically you fail to come up to the supposedly required standard of competence – short of driving straight into the wall during your test. Remember, driving school instructors can play an "important" role as middlemen in securing the co-operation of the licensing officer.

If all else fails and you really cannot hack it on the roads, you could always secure a diplomatic posting. Such positions have the immediate advantage of immunity from prosecution for vehicular high jinks in neighbouring states, and of course they also tend to come with a chauffeur. But if your chauffeur is South African, be sure to check how he got his licence.

Pounds and pence

Police vehicle pounds, where stolen vehicles are kept for owners to claim, are the least secure places for cars to be kept – worse, if possible, than wherever the vehicle in question was stolen in the first place.

Police officials are not well-paid professionals and unclaimed vehicles routinely get stripped of parts after they have been recovered. This usually leaves the owner in possession of a few bits of scrap and a headache with the insurance companies, who prefer to describe the wreck as a car and therefore decline to pay out. Some owners of recovered vehicles are, at least arguably, luckier: some vehicles are merely stamped with new numbers and issued with clearance certificates before being reregistered and going back into circulation.

The mysterious case of the disappearing docket

Pioneered by police of the old regime – where it was put to best use in political cases where police had to account for deaths in detention, or were called upon to investigate their colleagues – the disappearing docket has been enthusiastically adopted by the new South African order. There are occasional nods towards the old style of doing things – like the disappearance of a whole briefcase filled with evidence of police corruption after a mysterious and fatal accident involving a top investigator. However, nowadays the disappearing document PLB tends to have a more commercial flavour.

The purchase price for dockets from police officers and court officials of civil servants, the price can often be surprisingly reasonable. Even murder dockets sometimes cost as little as R1 000.

A variation on the disappearing docket has recently come strongly to the fore in the awarding of a third cellular licence, where scores of company records disappeared from the central registry in Pretoria before they could be scrutinised by the Office of the Auditor General. Perhaps it is this manifest flexibility offered by bureaucratic paperwork (as opposed to computer records, where it is difficult to claim that the hard drive is on loan) that makes the registrar of companies cling to this seemingly archaic method of notarisation in the face of technological advances.

Computer data bases are not sacrosanct. Particularly if you have contacts in the intelligence agencies, you can get them to break in a nd steal the whole computer. But most analysts would not see such practices as reaching the PLB threshold. Most would not rate this higher than BDB (Barely Defensible Behaviour), the kind of thing that involves a whole cycle of otherwise unnecessary PLB manoeuvres. (See also: Front companies.)

Crediting credit cards

The most common way of milking parastatals and other state agencies is through the creative use of company credit cards. Among other services available to the executive via the Gold Card (and now you know where it got that name) are: the purchase of groceries, the payment of private school fees, travel for self and family, visits to massage parlours and brothels, and so on.

Creative credit card usage is not, however, to be confused with corruption, as a top academic, caught unable to account for R160 000 on his magic plastic, pointed out. He insisted angrily that in being found guilty of credit card fraud, he had been cleared of corruption charges. Now that is PLB for you!

Sporting bets

Much in the news of late, and definitely not to be confused with match-fixing, "match forecasting" is a time-honoured PLB, and disgraced South African cricket captain Hansie Cronje is in good company. Australians Mark Waugh and Shane Warne blazed the trail years ago, themselves following apparently in the footsteps of Brits who invented the diversion. But never has a match been quite as precisely discussed as between Cronje and London bookie Sanjeev Chawla, where definite scores by individual players were discussed, and – a credit to Cronje's almost astrological prescience – almost as precisely fulfilled. Only feisty all-rounder Lance Klusener's manifest lack of more arcane skills than wielding the willow and hurling the kookaburra prevented an entirely accurate forecast.

And then there is soccer. The difference between a score of 1-0 and 1-1 in a professional soccer match can sometimes mean the difference between surviving in the league and ignominious relegation. One Professional Soccer League referee apparently felt the vicarious pang of disappointment so strongly he allowed a game to go on for fully 20 minutes after its scheduled close – then ended it the moment an equaliser was scored.

More generally, the outcomes of games are often discussed by the managers of the competing teams, routinely and in a collegial sort of way, resulting in subtle adjustments to likely outcomes. And of course to various bank balances.

Not that such practices are confined to what are generally regarded as team sports – as a pair of brothers, sharing not only their genes but also their competition identification numbers in sequence, reminded us in a pioneering case of PLB in the Comrades Marathon.

We will not even be dicussing horses or boxing in this place, but we do await with anticipation reports of pigeon fanciers weighing their birds down with shackles instead of tags to, well, help the competition.

Permitting work and work permits

Though widespread at every level of government, this particular species of PLB is most dazzlingly exploited by senior officials in the Department of Home Affairs who, by facilitating the issuing of work permits to foreign nationals of, say, Sudanese and West African origin, are able to put together basketball teams that literally tower over the opposition.

If you are not lucky enough to work for home affairs, but are still a senior civil servant, a little ingenuity still goes a long way. For instance a sinecure in the Department of Correctional Services can be put to excellent use by making playing fields and other facilities available to your private football team. And the prisoners? Ah, just throw them down a mineshaft if they get in the way.

Behind the front companies

Here is the nitty-gritty of PLB and the redistribution of assets. The front company is nothing new, and it was used to some effect by the agents of the old security forces in their efforts to privatise their own core business of murder and mayhem. But in the new dispensation, the obstacle that needs to be surmounted is this.

As a fiduciary public official you are often in a position to award lucrative contracts, but are barred by irritating legislation from also accepting them. Never fear. Family members can be roped in to set up shell companies (no experience in the relevant business needed). Friends or trusted employees can be given directorships.

But, with no meaningful legislation yet in place to ensure the identification of occult beneficiaries behind nominees, the preferred method these days is to hire an accountant to sign for your shares in companies tendering for contracts which you will be awarding.

There appears to be no particular pressure even to consider awarding the contract to the bidder who comes in with the lowest estimates. Quite the contrary! It is a PLB rule of thumb that he who bids double wins. (See: Commissioning.)

Bear in mind here that having secured the contract – and established yourself in the position of an occult beneficiary – your company does not actually have to do the work specified in the contract. The mere fact that you set up a housing company, for instance, and thereby promoted the cause of black empowerment, or a weapons company to promote employment, doesn't mean you know anything about building houses or manufacturing submarine communications systems, does it?

What you do in this eventuality is: you make a nod-and-a-wink kind of deal with people who do know how to build houses, but have been excluded from the contract because of their connections to the old political and economic order or, if you want to be blunt about it, their whiteness.

An elegant solution: they build the houses, you split the proceeds. This is where the practice of giving the job to the highest bidder makes particularly good sense in a PLB kind of way.

Commissioning procedures

In the arcane world of PLB opportunity, commissioning of programming on the national public airwaves can be turned into a variation of the public tender.

The step here is to bypass established commissioning procedures where far too many cooks – like financial managers and, especially, members of governing boards – can spoil the broth. You can always get the required authorisation later.

You then buy or commission programmes that never get used – or, if they do, seemingly get used by accident – at double the market price. If you are caught, you can claim Perfectly Legitimately that you lacked proper leadership. "Look," you might point out, "there are no signatures here from the people supposedly keeping an eye on things. What was I supposed to do? Not corruption, I reject that. Maybe mismanagement, I'll accept mismanagement. Okay?"

Meanwhile nobody thinks to ask, for example, where you got the money to buy that house, let alone put R3-million into refurbishing it.

Securing your pension and keeping your job

Why should the merely deceased stop being paid their state pensions? If you think this curtailment is unreasonable and unnecessary, you could follow the lead of enterprising entrepreneurs in the Eastern Cape and the Northern Province.

If you follow this route, you will, incidentally, also be scoring transformation brownie points, establishing as you would be a true and meaningful partnership between the public and the private sectors.

This how it goes: when a person passes on to greener pastures, rather than deleting that person from the official records of pension beneficiaries, you look to recycle rather than discard, and with the help of a Department of Welfare official, you simply replace the identifying fingerprint of the sadly missed pensioner with that of somebody who is still alive and in a position to use the pension payout. There is no good reason why any one pension entrepreneur should not collect 20 or even 50 such pensions every month, much to the benefit of the living (both in the public and the private sector), while, as they say, the dead look after the dead.

if the money gets heisted on the way to the payout point.

If you do not, on principle, object to working, another way of living better is to continue to receive a salary from the state while running your own business on the side. Interestingly this appears to be the PLB most favoured by teachers in state schools.

But for civil servants from the former homeland administrations, it can have its drawbacks: you need to invest in at least two jackets to hang, alternately, over the chair in your office to establish your continued presence. And it can also eat into your time, as you will have to make a point of being at the office for visits by ministers of state and other would-be-avenging dignitaries.

Unfortunately, the officially matching fingerprint will do you no good

Promising and delivering

Many a civil servant must have surveyed state assets like game parks and heritage sites, morosely pondering the essential unproductivity of such resources. But for a select and enlightened few, especially free thinkers in Mpumalanga and in the traditional authorities of KwaZulu-Natal, the answer has presented itself. The answer lies in the promissory note, whereby you pledge the future use of the resource. In exchange, the would-be entrepreneurs pay you some (usually seven-figure) consideration. Right now! And preferably offshore!

This particular PLB becomes even more legitimate if it is launched in partnership with public-spirited organisations like the youth leagues of political parties.

Jobs for pals

While some controls still exist over the appointment of permament officials in state departments and the civil service (and circumspection needs to be exercised if you want to employ your husband or wife, or brother or sister), the same is seldom true in the appointment of consultants. This then is, understandably, the preferred route for Perfectly Legitimate Nepotists, quite apart from the fact that consultants, because they are in theory uniquely qualified, can name their own price – and then double it.

So, to take a hypothetical instance, if you have a prospective employee who has demonstrated his entrepreneurial flair in unconventional ways, like using his position as minister of finance in his own country north of South Africa to privatise the state oil company in his own name, this is definitely the route to take. And it offers the added benefit of allowing him to bring his son in on the deal as well.

Pass one, pass all

More than one practitioner of PLB has been caught out in recent years for having not entirely earned academic qualifications, and no doubt more will follow. How much better, though, if the devotee of PLB did not have to forge or, well, amplify them in the first place?

Happily our education system seems to moving in just this enlightened direction. A R50 note passed to an underpaid teacher will often secure a glowing school report for a pupil who has failed the end-of-year examination. Of course, if you really want to do it the hard way, you can buy examination question papers before the exam is actually written.

Whistling in the dark

We all agree we have a wonderful Constitution, further reinforced by the provisions of the Open Democracy Act. But whatever you do in a world of a million shades of grey, do not take the notion of democratic rights too far and try to blow the whistle on PLB. If you do, experience has shown, you will almost certainly be accused of corruption.

April 21 2000

Contributors

Debra Aarons is associate professor in the Department of General Linguistics at the University of Stellenbosch.

Charlotte Bauer, a Nieman fellow circa 1997/98, is now an assistant editor at the Sunday Times.

Derek Bauer has turned into a tourism mogul, with 27 shops throughout the country selling high-quality tourist gear, souvenirs and curios, frequently adorned with his drawings of animals.

Julia Beffon is sports editor of the *Mail & Guardian*.

David Beresford is correspondent for *The Observer*. He is the author of *Ten Men Dead*, a book about the 1981 Irish hunger strike, and *The Dear Walter Papers*. He writes a regular column, *Another Country*, for the *Mail & Guardian*.

Shaun de Waal is literary editor of the *Mail & Guardian* and author of *These Things Happen*, a collection of short stories, and the graphic novelette *Jack Marks*.

Harry Dugmore is one-third of Rapid Phase (see below).

Cameron Duodu, former editor of *Drum West Africa*, is a veteran Africa commentator.

Marion Edmunds is a television producer on the investigative programme *Special Assignment*.

Steven Francis is one-third of Rapid Phase (see below).

Steven Friedman is director of the Centre for Policy Studies, an independent research centre, and author of the trade union history, *Building Tomorrow Today*.

Arthur Maimane, a veteran journalist, began his career on *Drum* in its heyday, made films in London and returned to South Africa to join first *The Weekly Mail* and then *The Star*, where he was managing editor. He is the author of a novel, *Hate No More*, and a non-fiction book due out in 2001.

Irwin Manoim, a founder of *The Weekly Mail* and its joint editor for a decade, has recently launched an Internet publishing company with Anton Harber (see Harber).

John Matshikiza is a freelance writer, playwright and film-maker and a columnist for the *Mail & Guardian*.

Jubie Matlou is a journalist for the *Mail & Guardian*.

Thami Mkwanazi went into business in the early 1990s after several years as a journalist and columnist for *The Weekly Mail*.

Evidence wa ka Ngobeni is a journalist for the *Mail & Guardian*.

Kit Peel is a freelance journalist.

John Perlman, long-time journalist and sportswriter, is presenter of *Morning Live* on SAfm.

Bridget Pitt (also known as the cartoonist, BP) is the author of the novel *Unbroken Wing*.

Ivor Powell is sporadically a member of the *Mail & Guardian* newsroom, occasionally a television reporter and the author of *Ndebele*, a book on art and politics, published by Struik.

Rant Boy is a pseudonym of stand-up comic Alyn Adams.

Rapid Phase is a sprawling media empire, created in 1992 by Harry Dugmore, Steven Francis and Rico Schacherl, then penniless artists and writers. Since their first *Madam and Eve* appeared in the *Mail & Guardian* they have published nine collections of the cartoon strip and devised a television series based on it. They have also become film-makers and Web magnates.

Michael Sarakinsky is a sociologist now teaching at the Institute for Adult Basic Education and Training at Unisa.

Mercedes Sayagues is the *Mail & Guardian*'s Zimbabwe correspondent.

Jonathan Shapiro, better known as Zapiro, is a political cartoonist whose work appears weekly in the *Mail & Guardian*, daily in *The Sowetan* and annually in best-selling collections.

Gus Silber is the author of several best-selling books on subjects ranging from the New South Africa *(It Takes Two to Toyi-Toyi)* to children and computers *(The Parent's Guide ...)*. He is also a feature movie scriptwriter, with credits that include Leon Schuster's *Panic Mechanic* and the comedy *Dazzle*.

Mungo Soggot is a journalist with the *Mail & Guardian*.

Stacey Stent is a freelance animator/cartoonist/artist doing print, Web and CD-ROM work for, among other organisations, the Multimedia Education Group and District Six Museum.

Rico Schacherl, a cartoonist of note, is one-third of Rapid Phase (see above).

Jack Swanepoel, aka Dr Jack, farmer, wildlife painter and former resident artist for South African National Parks, is the author of *Dr Jack's Illustrated South African Byrd Book*. His cartoons appear in a number of newspapers, including the *Mail & Guardian*.

Jeff Zerbst, aka Thomas Equinus, followed his PhD in the philosophy of religion from Wits University with the posts of associate editor of South African *Hustler* and editor of *Hustler* UK. He is now editor of Australian *Hustler*.